The Small Business
Start-Up
Guide

2nd Edition

A Surefire Blueprint
to Successfully Launch
Your Own Business

Hal Root and Steve Koenig

 Sourcebooks, Inc.
Naperville, IL

Published by: Sourcebooks, Inc.
P.O. Box 4410, Naperville, Illinois 60567-4410
(630) 961-3900
FAX: 630-961-2168

This publication is designed to provide accurate and authoritative information in regard to the subject matter covered. It is sold with the understanding that the publisher is not engaged in rendering legal, accounting, or other professional service. If legal advice or other expert assistance is required, the services of a competent professional person should be sought.

From a Declaration of Principles Jointly Adopted by a Committee of the American Bar Association and a Committee of Publishers and Associations

Library of Congress Cataloging-in-Publication Data

Root, Hal.
    The small business start-up guide / Hal Root and Steve Koenig.—2nd ed.
       p. cm.
    Includes index.
    ISBN 1-57071-221-2
    1. New business enterprises—United States—Handbooks, manuals etc.. I. Koenig, Steve. II. Title. III. Series.

Printed and bound in the United States of America.

VHG — 10 9 8 7 6 5

Contents

PART II: State Requirements

Introduction

The small business is the backbone of the American economy. In a sense, it always has been. From the first shopkeepers of the thirteen colonies to the local restaurateurs of today, small business has been the one constant economic force in America. Today, fully one half of all workers in the private sector are employed by the nation's twenty-two million small businesses.

Corporations, partnerships, and sole proprietors of every size and importance generate half of our country's Gross Domestic Product. Small Office/Home Office (SOHO) businesses are ever increasing parts of this business mix. The importance of small business is not lost on you because you have made the first crucial decision: to start one.

Chances are, you are one of the 50 percent of Americans employed by a large company, the government, agriculture, or a non-profit organization. Or, you are now unemployed and looking for a change. Whatever your reason, you have decided to purchase this book, and by doing so, you have decided to join the small business economic juggernaut. Maybe your business will be part-time and home-based. Maybe you will decide to chuck it all and go full-time, sinking all your time and money into it. Whatever you decide, you have picked our book to help guide you through the start-up, and we will do just that.

This second edition of *The Small Business Start-Up Guide* is a fact-filled account of the do's and don'ts of starting a small business in the late 1990s. As in the first edition, the pertinent information is presented without the clutter of gregarious psychological booster material. You can get that somewhere else. However, it is necessary to be serious and excited about your proposed business, which is why we wrote this book in a style that's easy to follow and quick to read. The fluff and repetition common to so many small business books is omitted, leaving you with "just the facts, ma'am."

Although intended for a beginner, even an established businessperson can use this as a reference guide, or better yet, give it to another potential entrepreneur to read. The more who know the basic, commonsense facts about starting a business, the better.

Since the first edition, there have been numerous changes in - laws, taxation, the government, society, and the economy. For example, home-based businesses have ballooned to over three million. Coupled with the nearly nine to ten million Americans who work at home (but for a company other than their own) you can see a definite trend.

Now Is the Time to Start Your Small Business

Right now is possibly the best time ever to start a small business. The availability of good business quality personal computers and software has never been better or cheaper. The fax, modem, Pentium-based PC, Windows programs, and the Internet all give small businesses a much more level playing field with the larger companies than ever before. Today, even the smallest business can generate a big business look and appearance with technology, software programs, and the Internet. Couple the information and technology booms with the excellent economy, low interest rates, current and future federal small business reform, and relative political/social stability and you get the perfect climate in which to start a small business. Because of all the changes in technology, the economy, communications, and govern-ment, this might be the best time ever to start a small business. We do not mean to deny the fact that every business faces immutable problems and challenges that remain constant over time, and with more people starting small businesses, especially home-based businesses, competition is fierce. But now is an excellent time to start a business.

Realizing the changes since 1994, when this book was first published, we have revised our book accordingly. The most important additions have been more information and sources of information, including Internet based sources. Complete, up-to-date information has been packed between the covers, and extensive revisions and additions of material, resources, information, requirements, and addresses now make this the one-stop compendium on starting a small business.

About This Book

Now a word about this book you will soon read. It is divided into three parts and three appendixes. PART I's twelve chapters deal with the preliminary tasks, research, and preparation needed to start a small business; the pros and cons of various business entities; how to actually start each type of entity; and useful start-up information about vital issues like insurance, taxes, and financing that can be used at start-up and while running the company.

PART II consists of a complete listing of the requirements of all fifty-one states and the District of Columbia for starting sole proprietorships, partnerships, limited liability companies, and corporations. Specific resources and services offered in each state are also listed, as are addresses and phone numbers of state and federal assistance centers.

Three appendixes conclude the book. Appendix A lists the Small Business Administration Publications. Appendix B has a list of the state sales and corporate tax rates. Finally, appendix C contains the Vital Start-Up Information Worksheet.

A Word of Caution

This book should in no way be considered a legal guide. NEVER, NEVER take legal advice from anyone but a lawyer. However, the information contained herein is factual and researched. Any omissions or errors are purely unintentional. The authors assume no responsibility for misinterpretation, unintentional error, or misprints. This is a guide to use along with the professional and legal help you seek. It is a very informative overview designed to get you thinking about the pitfalls and possibilities ahead. By recognizing the pros and cons of starting a small business, you will be better able to deal with the complexities of running your business later.

We say this, because in March of 1991, we incorporated as Root & Koenig, Inc. The process was filled with headaches, technicalities, and little problems that got larger. The entire process from seeing a lawyer, to getting the last document we needed, was an incredible two-and-a-half months. Some of this was due to bureaucracy, but most was due to our own ignorance of the proper procedures and requirements.

We would have given anything for a straightforward, concise guide to incorporation and starting-up a business. We did not need motivation or books describing trends in businesses. We needed solid information without all the accompanying fluff. Unfortunately, all we found at that time was the fluff.

The local bookstores stocked only motivational or trendy books. While the books might have been relevant to some, to us they were simply impediments to finding the information we needed. The solid how-to on starting a business was elusive, so we decided that we would share with you the things we found out first hand—the hard way. What we have produced can be used by the novice business person as a handy reference guide to the many details necessary to start a successful small business in the closing years of the century.

Acknowledgements

We would like to thank the staff at Sourcebooks for help and consul in the harried drafting of this second edition. Particular thanks go to Dominique Raccah, the publisher who first gave this book a chance, and to Todd Stocke, whose editing suggestions and comments were invaluable and much appreciated. He is what an editor should be. We are indebted to John Flanagan at the Indianapolis SBA for sources of information and advice;. to Matthew Blair at the Community Development Corporation in Fort Wayne for information on city-level small business development programs and financing; and to Mark Wilder and Jeff Sprinkle at Norwest Bank Indiana N.A. for financial and lending information. Also, thanks go out to the many local, state, and federal government agencies that responded to our requests for information, some within days of our initial requests. Additionally, we would like to thank the many individuals at libraries, bookstores, businesses, agencies, think tanks, and banks who provided much of the information for this revised edition.

We hope this second edition of *The Small Business Start-Up Guide* is useful in the formation of your small business, whatever its size. Wishing you luck, success, and profits!

—Hal Root and Steve Koenig

Part 1

Business Start-Up

Chapter 1

Are You Really Ready?

Questions to Ask Yourself at Start-Up

By purchasing this book, you have decided to join the swelling ranks of small business owners and entrepreneurs. The time for procrastination is over. You have decided your business idea is feasible, and now you begin the process of actually starting that small business. We think that's great.

But before you actually proceed with the start-up procedure, we feel you should take some time to prepare yourself for what is going to happen. Starting your small business will seem easy compared to what happens next—making that business work. While this book is devoted to starting, rather than running, a small business, we feel now—in the beginning—is the time to ask yourself some vital questions about yourself, your ideas, and business in general.

Maybe you have already done that, maybe you have asked every imaginable question of yourself and your business. that's good. But chances are you have not asked enough questions. No one can ever question a business idea enough.

For instance, in 1975 there was no personal computer market. However, a handful of innovators and forward-thinking computer enthusiasts believed that people would want a computer in their homes. The result—well, you know the result. Had those people decided there was no market for home PC's, Apple, Microsoft, and scores of firms would not exist. Nothing is disingenuous or wrong about starting a business in uncharted territory or with lingering questions, but by asking questions and then researching the answers—or thinking about them—you can highlight and eliminate many problem areas before you start. Then, while you are running your business, you can tackle the lingering questions.

It is suicide to go into business without being motivated or prepared for the responsibilities. Believe it or not, being motivated does not mean not having doubts. Everyone has doubts, even successful entrepreneurs. It is human nature. Rather, proper motivation means confronting and conquering your doubts before turning to the fulfillment of your dreams. Your motivation has to last before, during, and after you start your business. If you can accomplish this, you will be on your way to success and farther away from being one of the seventy thousand failed small businesses each year and the even greater number of bankruptcies.

But it is not enough to be motivated—to conquer your doubts and jump into the business arena. You also have to possess motivation. That's, you must have an underlying desire, need, or want in order to keep the fire of your dream alive, especially during the lean start-up times.

Whatever your motivation—you hate the boss, you have a great product or skill, or you just want to work for yourself—now is the time to solidify it by questioning it.

• Am I ready for this; can I handle the responsibilities?

The answer to this question will most likely be yes. However, make sure it is an honest "yes" before beginning your journey. There is nothing wrong with admitting that you are not ready and that starting a business is too much for you to handle at a certain time (one reason people form partnerships). So if you do not think you are ready, step back, analyze the reasons you believe you are not ready and take corrective action. Maybe you need some time to distance personal problems from your start-up. Maybe you need to do more research or planning first. If you just do not have the money, try to find a way to get it. Whatever the answer, you will be glad you confronted this question early on. Nothing is worse than external or internal distractions that keep you from devoting time to your business.

Can you handle extreme pressure from your business, your family, and your friends, all of whom will complain that they do not see you enough? You must be prepared for this challenge more than any other, because it is personal in nature.

- ## Do I have the staying power to become a business person in today's high-pressure, highly competitive small business world?

Being a modern American small businessperson is not easy. All companies, regardless of size, must change and adapt to their environments and to current trends in order to survive and flourish. Staying put does not win you the race. Can you, as a small businessperson, change and accept new ideas or methods in order to keep or gain market share?

Initially you will have a hectic and possibly frustrating time starting your small business. After all, you have to sell your product or service, deliver it to your customers' satisfaction, and maintain the momentum of your start-up. Then comes more twelve and fourteen hour-workdays, seven-day work weeks, and self-sacrifices that must be endured for whatever period of time it takes you to be successful. But once "there"—wherever it is your goals take you—you must continually strive for more success. This is what staying power is all about. Those who can change and adapt, and work hard at it, will be successful. Those that cannot, will work for other people their whole lives.

With more and more Americans starting small businesses, competition is increasing and market shares are decreasing. Your success will depend partly on how you deal with this reality and all other economic and social trends that affect small business.

- ## Am I prepared to compete with the other 800,000 people starting businesses this year?

Many businesses fail in the first few years for a variety of reasons. The Small Business Administration reports that around seventy-thousand—about one in ten—start-up businesses fail every year due to varying causes. Nearly fifty-thousand businesses go bankrupt.

By knowing the odds before beginning a business, you can develop a plan to beat those odds and compete.

As we mentioned above, hard work and persistence are important. But so are other things such as timing, initiative, pricing, product, marketing, the economy, and luck. Those same criteria affect every business in America, though not always in the same ways. Failed businesses collapse for many reasons. Any set of factors can adversely affect a small business: a faltering economy; a poor marketing scheme; a poor product or service; a saturated marketplace; or lack of financing, experience, or desire. Even personal problems such as a divorce or health problems can threaten the survival of your business.

Since so many people are starting businesses, especially small office, home office (SOHO) businesses, your competition is fierce. While not all are starting your type of business, the proliferation of small businesses means more small businesses are going after scarce consumer dollars. You have to compete for those dollars against free-trade laws that give foreign companies greater access to American markets, against small businesses with more start-up capital, and against smarter, more informed people. In short you are up against a lot, but the rewards of success are very sweet.

For you to succeed, you have to take on those hundreds of thousands of other entrepreneurs and beat them. You have to win. Why? Because that's your dream.

The answers to these questions should reveal whether you are ready to really think about your business structure. Even if you have some doubts, and you will, you probably will begin the process of going into business. Your small business will be a learning experience no doubt, but it need not be traumatic as long as you plan your course and confront your obstacles. You cannot know *everything* up front, but resolving the *important* issues early on will be a great benefit later.

Now, the next set of questions is our "Who, What, Where, Why, When, and How" section. As you answer these next questions, you will begin to see how much or how little you know about your business. If your answers disappoint you, take corrective actions. Use creative methods and resources to research the answers. Find out what you need to do if your answer to a question is "I don't know." Find the solutions before you go farther.

These questions, as well as your own that you will think up, are good starting points to beginning a business. There is no real order to these questions and that's purposeful. Just ask and answer them in any order you like. Some you can skip, because they may not pertain to you.

Who

- Who are my potential employees?
  - Do I need any?
  - What skills should I look for in employees?
  - How will I get them, what resources will I use? (Temp agencies, want ads, etc.)
  - What is the composition of the local labor force?
- Who are my potential customers?
  - How can I ensure customers are attracted and stay attracted?
  - How will I get these customers?
  - Is my customer base general or specific in nature?
- Who are my competitors?
  - How will I compete with them: price, quality, service, location?
  - Are they too competitive or too entrenched?
  - Are they successful?
  - What are their weaknesses?
  - Is the market oversaturated?
- Who will be my investors, partner(s), or company officers?
  - Do I need partners?
  - Do I work better alone? Can I work alone?
  - How do I pick a partner?
  - Should I have general or limited partners?
  - Will they be committed to the business?
  - Will I make the supreme effort to make good use of investors' capital?

What

- What is my product or service?
  - Have I sold, made, or offered these products or services in the past?
  - How am I different? How will I differentiate my service or product?
  - Is it different, unique, or better than the competitions?
  - How I pick supply and service vendors?
  - Is there a market for these services or products?
  - How do I fulfill customers' orders or requests? What is my distribution channel?
  - Do I have confidence that what I am making, providing or selling is quality?
- What compensation do I offer any employees I may have?
  - Do I take a salary?
  - Do I know how to do payroll?
  - How many employees can I afford at different salaries?
  - Can I attract quality employees with my offered wages?
  - Can I use non-pay incentives like comp time or stock options?
  - Do I know what competitors are paying employees?
  - Should I combine pay with bonuses?
- What benefits can I offer?
  - Do I need to offer benefits?
  - What, if any, benefits can I afford?
  - Are there associations or small business co-ops that share group benefits? If so, what are they?
  - Regardless of employees, do I personally need vacation time, health coverage, or a pension?
- What sources of help are available to me?
  - Can my local or state government offer start-up assistance?
  - What start-up resources does the Small Business Administration have that I can use?

- What magazines, radio and TV programs, private companies, or national small business organizations are available to me?

Where

- Where will I buy or lease an office, store, warehouse, or plant?
    - Can I start with a home office?
    - Can I meet zoning requirements at home?
    - How much space do I need?
    - What office and computer equipment do I need?
    - Can I work at home with no interruptions?
    - Will I need a separate phone line? A post office box? An answering service?
    - Can I afford office space?
- Where will I get start-up funding?
    - Can I obtain a loan at a bank or credit union? Will the institution loan money for a start-up?
    - Do they lend to SOHO businesses?
    - Am I willing to use my savings and investments?
    - Will family and friends invest with me?
    - Can I get development capital from the Small Business Administration or other state and local government entities?
    - Do I qualify for minority or women-owned business loans, programs, and/or grants?
    - Should I try a venture capitalist or an angel investor?
- Where do I want to be (in life) in five, ten, fifteen, twenty years? (This is a personal as well as a business question. Answer it and the following questions for yourself and your business).
    - What are my short-term goals?
    - What are my long-term goals?
    - Are my ultimate goals financial or satisfaction-based?
    - How will my business goals adversely affect my family life?
    - Are my goals realistic?

- How will I evaluate my success?
- What if I do not achieve my goals—what will I do?

Why

- Why should I choose a sole proprietorship, partnership, limited liability company, or corporation? (Also, what are the advantages/disadvantages of each?)
  - How big do I need to be to start out?
  - What aspects of each entity appeals to me?
  - What tax, regulatory, and/or licensing issues will affect my choice of entity?
  - Do I need to consider the liability protection offered by a corporation or limited liability company?
- Why should I go into business in the first place?
  - What are my real reasons and motivations? Are they personal, professional, or other?
  - Are my reasons supportable, i.e., am I doing this for positive rather than negative reasons?
  - Do I want to make a lot of money? Or am I in it for the freedom aspects?

When

- When should I start my business?
  - Is the economy—local, regional, state, national—good?
  - Should I work my current job while starting the business?
  - Is my business a growth industry?
  - Do I know when the right time is?
- When will I find time for family and friends? (We have restated this point for emphasis.)
  - Can I afford the social costs of starting a business?
  - Is it possible to let them work with me in the business?
  - Am I prepared for the loneliness of going it alone?

How

- How will I promote my business and/or product/service?
  - What choice of media should I use for advertising?
  - Can I get free publicity?
  - Can I sponsor teams, programs, or events?
  - Should I advertise in the yellow pages?
  - Can I use the Internet to my advantage?
  - How can networking at small business organizations and the Chamber Of Commerce help me?
- How much start-up capital will I need?
  - What are my initial fixed costs?
  - What will be my eventual fixed and variable costs?
  - Can I get assistance to determine my start-up needs?
- How do I manage my business?
  - How is payroll, accounting, human resource management, regulatory paperwork, tax filing, billing, and communication done in the business world? Do I know how to do all of these, especially if I have a SOHO business?
  - Do I know an accountant, lawyer, or SCORE officer who can help me plan for these eventualities?
  - What software can help me?

Hopefully, you have been able to ask and answer many of these questions. And hopefully, you have come up with dozens of others specifically related to your situation and business. A worksheet is included at the end of this chapter for you to write questions and answers on. Feel free to photocopy it and use it for your Q & A sessions.

In addition to these questions, the Small Business Administration has a list of thirty-one Most Asked Questions. These questions are asked by small businesspeople and answered by the SBA. It is an excellent resource. It is on the SBA Web site at the following Internet address *www.sbaonline.sba.gov.*

Asking and then answering these and future questions is the most vital thing you can do at this stage. If you go into business thinking you have all the answers and do not need to know what the questions were, you will end up a failed business from the start.

These questions can be asked and answered in order to help shape your initial business plan and influence your start-up operations. Chapter three will explore research and start-up planning and contains useful information on how to find answers to many of the questions you ask. Then you will use the answers as foundations to the various parts of your plan which is explained in chapter four. Here you will learn how they can be integrated into your business plan.

No doubt you might have some lingering questions that seem to defy answers. That's okay. As long as the bulk of your important questions go answered, you will be in a great position for your start-up. You will have answers and rock solid self-motivation that will be a driving force behind your business start-up. And proper motivation ensures that you will stick to your plans with the discipline necessary in small business.

Worksheet: Questions & Answers

Q._____

_____

A._____

_____

_____

Q._____

_____

A._____

_____

_____

Q._____

_____

A._____

_____

_____

Q._____

_____

A._____

_____

_____

The Great Eight Steps

Eight Steps to Start-Up Success

After you get the itch to start a business, the cycle begins to take on a life of its own. You decide you have a product or service that will appeal to a segment of the market. Next you decide to start a business.

After that you have to begin the process of starting the business, which includes research, business plans, filing forms and obtaining licenses, and finally conducting business. By following a guide, you can eliminate uncertainty about what steps to take. This smoothness will allow you to then concentrate on running your business after all the requirements of start-up have been completed. If your start-up is successful, it will impart that much more confidence in you as you begin business. This might seem trite, but a bad experience in the beginning can taint your whole operation.

The process of starting a small business, from idea to entity, can be broken into a series of stages or steps. Although no two start-ups are quite the same—each is unique in its own way—most will follow a set course. This chapter describes such a course—In this case, our eight step start-up guide.

We have broken the process into the following eight easy steps that you can use as guidelines, while you actually start your business. The idea is to follow each step in order, thus maintaining organization and eliminating possible confusion. Each step builds upon the process until, by the final one, you are actually in business.

This eight step process is generic in nature and meant to cover every type of start-up from sole proprietors to corporations. Obviously, some of the steps will not have the same bearing on certain entities as they will on some of the others. For instance, a corporation will probably develop a much more extensive business plan than a simple sole proprietorship will. Conversely, a sole proprietor may not necessarily need to consult a lawyer or an accountant. The key with this guide is to use it as a flexible, all-purpose list. If one step does not pertain to you, skip it.

The Eight Great Steps are: Product/Service Generation and Research; Research Your Idea; Develop a Business Plan; Consult a Lawyer and an Accountant; Determine Organization Type; Seek Government Help; Start Your Business; and Seek Sources of Financing.

These steps will serve as a guide to the rest of this book, as many of the steps are basically broken into chapters. And the steps are a further impetus to complete thorough research on your business and the federal and state governments' business requirements.

To aid you, we have included a worksheet with this chapter. It is the eight step process, a worksheet intended to help you follow the steps in order, to make notes where needed, and to check off each completed step. In appendix C is another worksheet that might help you note information and vital statistics for your business. This information can be used in a later chapter when you determine what entity to become.

The Great Eight Steps to Business Success

Step One: Product/Service Generation and Research

This step is where you will determine what product or service you have decided to offer consumers. For many of you, you have already done this. If not, you can do it now. Even if you have done it, it is now time to hone the idea and shape the actual identity of the product or service.

If your business will be a service, define what exact services you will offer and how. For instance, if you decide to open a clothing store, you must decide what type of clothing you will sell. You have to decide where you will sell it and how you will obtain the clothes for resale. If you open an accounting firm, you need to define what services you will offer: general services for the whole market or specific services for small market niches like tax accounting or business accounting. In short, prepare an organized outline of every part of the service (this is different from the business plan discussed later). Know what you are going to provide as a service and how you plan on providing it.

If your business is product driven, you must do one of two things: write a prospectus and make a model of it so that you and others see what it is you are making or contract a company to make a model. Either way, you must have a physical example of your product and a statement of what it will do. Again, that's what the product prospectus will accomplish. This is simply a short report on your product, how it is made, its uses and how it is better than similar existing ones. If it is a unique or new product, you might have to obtain a patent or trademark. See chapter twelve for the appropriate addresses.

Time. This may take weeks, months, or even years, but it is a crucial step. If you are developing a product, make sure you offer the best you can; it may take more time, but it will be financially well worth it.

Step Two: Research Your Idea

You can never have too much information, especially in the competitive world of small business. This vital step is intended to allow you to sharpen your knowledge of business and your chosen field.

While you are honing your idea, write to anyone and everyone you can think of for information. This includes the Small Business Administration, the Internal Revenue Service, state and local government entities, trade organizations, small business organizations, and any other resources. You can ask for a list of their publications, and services and products relevant to your small business idea (and for start-ups in general). A variety of useful sources and their addresses or phone numbers is listed in chapter twelve.

Gather this information, and begin pouring over it in anticipation of writing your business plan. Some of the information might also influence the final shape of your service or product.

Your research should be conducted in accordance with the questions asked in the first chapter. These can be used as a basis for general research on all aspects of business. Additionally, ask your own questions, and provide your own resources for answering them. Chapter three explains a variety of research resources and unique ideas. The results of steps one and two will culminate in a business plan.

Time. This might also take weeks, months, or even years, but it too is a vital step that should be given ample personal resources. It may take up to a month to order and receive SBA, IRS and other publications and information, so do it early in the process. While waiting, you can meet with local resources such as SCORE officers or local businesses and suppliers.

Step Three: Develop a Business Plan

This is a very important step and one you must do regardless of the size of the plan. The importance and scope of your plan depends on several factors, but all businesses should develop one.

A detailed business plan outlines your business start-up and the first six months to one year of operation. It will also include projections for three, five, or ten years down the road. This plan is your "blueprint" to success that in essence will guide your every business decision for the foreseeable future. You will want to be careful and thorough in its preparation.

The business plan is discussed in more detail in chapter four, and its various parts are explained there. Each of these defines and molds your business concept in one way or another. By thoroughly preparing each section, you will obtain that blueprint, which will also serve as a springboard to obtaining financing.

The size, type, and nature of your business will determine the depth and scope of your plan. The SBA, and in particular, its SCORE program, may be able to lend technical and practical advice to you in this area. Contact the SBA office in your area for more information. In addition, there are companies that provide consulting services to businesses covering marketing, personnel, finance, etc. However, the small business or the SOHO business these services might be too expensive.

With initiative, hard work, and patience this step will produce a written business plan for your small business.

Time. Again, this depends on the above mentioned factors. For a SOHO business, you might need to spend two weeks to one month on your plan. For larger businesses, a month to several months may be needed. Some people even spend a year writing and rewriting their plans until they are as professional as possible. This step should be done after one and two, but really can be done concurrently or as you gather the information from your research. And it might also overlap some steps that follow.

Step Four: Consult a Lawyer and an Accountant

You may need a lawyer and an accountant, if only for consultations on legal and tax issues. They can be of great help in many areas, especially when it comes to dealing with government regulations and small business legal issues. The SOHO may not need any consultations except when issues of zoning or regulations come up. If you intend to form any other entity, you might want to see an accountant for tax consultations and a lawyer for specific legal advice on regulations, state requirements, and licensing information.

Try visiting business lawyers and accountants who handle small businesses. They may have more detailed information for you. Additionally, if you cannot afford either, some communities have a low-cost business incubator or quasi-governmental business consulting centers that offer assistance.

If you need to consult either professional, keep in mind these specific questions.

Ask Both

- Is my choice of organization type right, in your opinion?

Ask an Attorney

- What forms need to be filed for certain entity types? Make a list of them and ask him or her to explain the purpose of each.
- What zoning or commerce regulations are there in my chosen field of business?
- Are there any other local restrictions?
- What services can you offer after I start my business? And what are your fees?

Ask an Accountant

- What is the tax effect of various entities?
- What taxes do I need to pay in various entity types?
- When do I need to pay them?
- How do I pay them?
- How should I handle accounting?
- When should my accounting year begin and end?

These are by no means exhaustive.

If you have it ready—and you should—take your business plan to the lawyer and accountant if you need to see either. This will give them a better understanding of your business. Part of the reason you may need to see an attorney and/or accountant is to determine which business entity to become. Both can offer practical advice on this issue. Once given, you can use that information in step five.

Time. Go after you have your business plan. A few days is all that's usually necessary although you may decide to wait until you are 100 percent ready. If you need a lawyer to handle an incorporation, you will want to get a list of fees and services. You might also have to see an attorney or accountant after step five as well.

Step Five: Determine Organization Type

The next step is to decide what entity is best for your business. Although some states differ, most will offer the following listed organizational types in order of simplest to most complex: sole proprietor, general partnership, limited partnership, limited liability company, and corporation. Corporations can be either C (regular) or S (sub-chapter S), profit or non-profit. Generally you will want a for-profit company however.

Determining your business entity depends on many factors including tax liability and rates, legal liability needs, business size, business type, capital (lack or possession of), personal preferences, needs, and/or future business plans. When you sit down to determine your business, think about what you will be doing and what types of business entity best protects your interests with the minimum of government interference and taxation.

Low requirements are demanded of sole proprietors and partnerships, while limited liability companies and corporations have more requirements and legal obligations. Each type is examined in chapter five, where a list of pluses and minuses rates each entity type. Your lawyer and accountant can help you make this decision if you are still confused.

SOHO businesses are often the simplest business entities because their needs are the simplest. However, if you start an at-home business, be aware that you may need liability protection or the structure offered by a more complex business entity. Although there are requirement and cost differences between simple and complex entities, you should not sacrifice your business needs for simplicity or cost's sake. A worksheet in chapter five will help you make this decision.

Time. Be sure to research the types of organization, and take all the time you need. It may take a day or two or up to a week. This can be done concurrently with the steps above but you may want to wait to make the final decision after you have consulted professionals.

Step Six: Seek Government Help

After researching, writing your business plan, consulting professionals, and solidifying your business entity, you might want to pursue this optional step. A consultation with your local SBA or SCORE office might provide you with further sources of government assistance.

A SOHO business might pursue this step in lieu of seeing accountants or lawyers, if only to save money. Additionally, these government small business organizations can inform you how to obtain loans, start-up assistance, local information, minority and women business assistance, and practical advice, especially from SCORE officers. Chapter twelve lists the various SBA programs and services. Appendix A has a list of SBA publications.

These agencies deal with small and new businesses every day and can provide you with expert and friendly advice. At SCORE, retired executives will try to assist you and answer questions or concerns you might have.

Time. Do this the same week as you see the lawyer and the accountant, or in lieu of either. It might help if you know what entity you will become before seeing them. However, they may also be able to help you make that decision.

Step Seven: Start Your Business

After you have all the facts, become the business. You will now know what type of business entity you are set to become. The next thing to do is file the necessary forms and pay any filing fees and/or licensing fees. The listings in PART II give state requirements for each type of entity. Generally, you will do five things in this step:

1. File for a Federal Tax ID number
2. Prepare and file any required state forms or licenses
3. Register with your state revenue department
4. Check local requirements/licensing
5. Set up a bank account

If you need a lawyer to assist you, he or she will prepare the forms when you first visit. After a second visit he or she will ask you for specific information including company name, officers, etc. A week or two later, the forms should be ready for you to sign. They will probably be mailed to you. Read them over carefully, and do not be afraid to ask the attorney questions. Always make sure either you or your lawyer fills out any necessary state forms such as sales tax ID number forms, withholding forms, and licensing paperwork. In addition, apply for a Federal Employer ID number by filing form SS-4. This number is used to identify you as an employer for purposes of tax reporting.

Your state revenue department will likely register you for withholding tax, sales and use tax, and other necessary taxes. Most likely, this is done with one or two forms. Local requirements range from city or county business licenses and permits to city or county tax registration. Your local officials will help you through the process. Usually you will contact the county clerk, recorder, or city clerk or revenue office. Your local yellow pages will include the proper local numbers to call.

The final stage of this step is to get an account at a local bank or credit union. Shop around for value and services. The fees and services will vary from bank to bank and between large and small banks. Use a reputable bank that you feel comfortable with. Your bank will be important to you, so it is important to have a good relationship with it.

Time. Unfortunately, this is a variable time, and may take up to one month for the whole process to be finished. You can speed it along by using expedited services many states offer for an additional fee. The bank account must be obtained after you start business.

Step Eight: Seek Sources of Financing

This is the final step, because no one except your mother will invest in your business if it is not a legal entity.

Once you have become your small business you can begin the process of obtaining funding. Several sources abound and are fully discussed in chapter eight. Banks, the SBA, private foundations, angel investors, venture capitalists, stockholders, and friends and family are all possible sources of financing.

Since this step is done after starting your business entity, you will have your business plan and business structure established. You will want to look, act, and be professional in every aspect of this endeavor. This will allow potential investors a look at your plans. Start-up funding is very hard to get though, so you may have to use sources near to you—yourself, friends, family—until you grow enough to be attractive to a bank or investor. Selling stock by direct public offering (DPO, the first offering is often referred to as an initial public offering—IPO) is one way a new small business can get funding, and it is growing in popularity. Most states have specific laws and requirements to follow if you do a DPO, and you should consult an attorney before doing so.

In your search for funding do not forget to stay encouraged even when you are rejected (and you will be). The bank that turns you down today may give you a loan after you have proven you can run your business.

Time. Varies. You may or may not get a loan or start-up capital. This depends on your plan, and who you see for capital.

Technically there is one more step: Start Operating Your Business! As soon as you can, get things rolling. The old adage that time is money is true especially for a small business. As a small business owner, you will soon discover that fact.

Worksheet: Great Eight Steps Checklist

Check off the box as you complete each step.

☐ Step One: Product/Service Generation and Research
Date Completed:_____

☐ Step Two: Research Your Idea
Date Completed:_____

☐ Step Three: Develop a Business Plan
Date Completed:_____

☐ Step Four: Consult a Lawyer and an Accountant
Date Completed:_____

☐ Step Five: Determine Organization Type
Date Completed:_____

☐ Step Six: Seek Government Help
Date Completed:_____

☐ Step Seven: Start Your Business (File all necessary forms)
- Federal Identification Number Reg. Date
  Completed:_____
- State/Local Business Registration. Date
  Completed:_____
- State Tax Registration. Date
  Completed:_____

☐ Step Eight: Seek Sources of Financing
Date Completed:_____

Notes:_____

_____

_____

_____

_____

_____

Beginning the Process

Researching and Documenting
Your Start-Up Needs

This chapter begins the process of going into business. You are not in business yet, but after its completion, you will be on your way to the most important step, the business plan. Additionally, you will have discovered answers to questions that have gone unanswered.

Researching everything about your chosen business, from regulations to start-up requirements to sources of capital to suppliers is vital. Much of your research will be predicated on the simple question: What don't I know? In chapter one you were asked to answer a battery of questions. Hopefully, you came up with many more of your own. Chances are you do not have the answers to all of the questions. That's okay, because you can now research for those answers, statistics, and information.

Prior to forming your business, you should be prepared to spend several hours in the library, at the bookstore, on the Internet, at the Small Business Administration, SCORE, or other government agencies, at trade shows, conventions, association meetings, the Chamber Of Commerce, business development centers, and if possible, in stores, offices, or factories, researching your chosen business.

Or, if you are unsure about which business you want to be in, research several. You can make a list of all of them with good and bad points listed, then choose the one in which you think you can be most successful. You see, the initial research into your business begins with your idea. Most of you already have an idea in mind. Coming up with that idea might have been easy—you are in the industry you have chosen for your business, or you specialize in something that you feel will make a good business. For others who are unsure, a variety of resources exist to research various business ideas and their start-up requirements. Chapter twelve has many of these listed.

After your idea is developed, there are six steps we recommend in order to thoroughly research your business.

1. List Your Personal Goals First

Yes, you may have done this in chapter one, but sit down again and write what you want to do with your life. List your likes, dislikes, and goals (financial and family). Take a great deal of time with this and be thorough. The more you are willing to admit about (and to) yourself, the more you will channel that into your business goals. Be sure to list where you want to be in three, five, and ten years.

2. List Your Business Goals

Write what you want your business to become in the short and long-term. Ask yourself the questions from chapter one to help shape and mold those goals. Be sure to include questions you have developed on your own. You may not have answers to all of the questions or you may be dissatisfied with some of the answers and that will spur you to research.

3. Compare Your Goals

Compare the goals in item one with those in item two, and determine which businesses will most be able to satisfy your personal and professional goals. Often, your personal goals will dictate your professional goals.

4. Begin Your Research

Here you simply use or go to any of the resources listed later in this chapter. The different methodologies of research and fact finding should be fairly all-encompassing. Do not limit yourself to one type of research or one source for your information. Remember, you can never have enough information. Your research will be done to answer your questions, support your business idea, and provide you with complete information for current or future use.

5. Collect the Data and Information

After you have researched, gather your data together in one place, and take some time alone or with your business partner(s) to go over it. Remember, this information will not only help your business but also you. Yes, your research should provide answers to soothe your nervousness or apprehensions. It will also provide the framework for your all-important business plan, covered in the next chapter.

6. Re-Research

After you have gathered your information you may discover you need still more facts or answers. Why? Because your research will inevitably raise new questions that need new answers. Do not be alarmed, this is normal. Any process as involved as starting a business is bound to be complex and time consuming, and you must be flexible enough to work with that complexity. If that means burning the midnight oil pursuing more answers, do it. In the end, you will be happy you did.

Now that you have a template for your research, let's discuss some ways to go about this.

Researching can be accomplished in many different ways and with many different resources. Luckily, we live in the communication and information age, where the click of a few computer keys and the movement of a mouse can bring a wealth of information to our computer screens. Information is literally at your fingertips waiting to be had. The resources and methods listed below are diverse and in some cases unique. This should give you an edge on your small business start-up competitors. Many more specific sources of help are listed in chapter twelve.

How to Gather Information

- Visit your local library, bookstore, or magazine stand. These resources contain further resources that will greatly aid your search. Many libraries have business sections and most are computerized, which makes inter-library searching and loans easier. A variety of books and magazines on business await you at your bookstore. Some publications and books are listed in chapter twelve.

- Use the Small Business Administration's many agencies and programs. Along with the SBA, other government entities provide business information.

- Talk to a retired executive at the Service Corps of Retired Executives (SCORE), an organization funded by the SBA. These men and women can be very helpful and can use their experience and knowledge to aid your research.

- Use demographic data such as traffic counts, population statistics, crime data, census figures, tax rates, buying trends, etc.

- Conduct market studies and surveys. You can do this yourself either formally or informally to obtain feedback on your product or service. If you have the money, you can hire a firm to do this.

- Spy. That's right. If you want to know about prices at another store or how many customers a competitor has, simply visit the store and walk around. (Please, do not wiretap or bug your competitors.)

- Work in your chosen small business before starting one. Nothing beats experience to show you the ropes.

- Attend trade shows, expos, and business fairs. These are excellent sources of information and personal con-tacts and allow you to scan what is out there competing with you.

- Network with colleagues, friends, or associates. Everyone knows someone else who can help them with some aspect of their business. Use these friends, associates, and their knowledge to your best advantage. Most will be glad to give advice or help.

- Visit local colleges to see if they have any resources that might help you in your start-up. Many campuses are sites of the SBA program's Small Business Development Centers. Colleges may also have some demographic and economic data for you.

- Use job interviews and resumes to evaluate the employee pool in your community.
- Follow the local and national news. Keep abreast of trends and fads. Often your local papers contain a wealth of small business news in your community.
- Talk to members of your local Chamber of Commerce. Again, they will probably be open to helping you along. They were once in your situation.
- Use the Internet to open the door to a Pandora's box of business and government Web sites. The beauty of the Internet is that one site often leads to another. It is an excellent source of addresses and information. Use the Internet yellow pages as well.
- Talk to entrepreneurs who have started their own businesses for advice, information, and even encouragement. Many small business owners will gladly tell you what they went through.
- Use your local yellow pages. Also, large city phone books have a wealth of phone numbers for companies, services, and products in their yellow pages.
- Write to companies and request information on how they started out.
- Buy competitors' goods to compare to yours, and make notes on how they advertise.
- Talk to competitors' former employees if you know of any. They may give you insight into how the competition operates.
- Brainstorm.Use your own noggin and that of a partner, friend, or spouse to come up with your own unique answers and information. Personal questions can often be answered very effectively this way.
- Attend continuing education courses taught by local universities. These refresher courses may contain information or contacts well worth your time.
- Utilize private companies or private business organizations and associations. Many associations exist for small businesses, and they are often open to dispensing help and information. Join a few, and use their resources for your research.

- Utilize trade publications. Most trades and businesses have newspapers, publications, or newsletters. These may be of assistance.
- Use banks, accountants, and attorneys as sources of information. Talk to a banker experienced in business lending—he or she can provide valuable insight.
- Visit your local government's economic development department for information on finances and available programs.
- Listen to talk radio business programs, and watch business shows on televisions.
- Join barter exchanges to exchange goods and services via barter. Akin to networking.
- Use a business consultant. Again, expensive, but if you have the money, a consultant might be able to help you start your business on a great footing.
- Purchase programs and software from business and entrepreneurial sources. These range from how-to-start specific business guides to business law manuals to cassette programs on motivation.
- Use minority and women's groups resources. Often minority and women's organizations (especially women's business groups) are eager to help those coming up through the small business ranks like they once did.
- Business think tanks can offer information. A few are listed in chapter twelve.

Be sure to mull over government publications and statistics related not only to your chosen businesses, but the economy as a whole. The whole economy does affect you, no matter how small you are. Most popular consumer magazines carry a potpourri of items useful to the investor, corporate-level executive, and even mid-level businesspeople. You will not find much about small business on a regular basis, though consumer publications often profile smaller businesses and report on small business trends. Also, these publications provide you with a pulse on the economy, society, trends in trade and finance, and successful corporate businesspeople. With small businesses proliferating, many are including more information on small businesses (even SOHOs.)

If you can satisfactorily answer the motivational questions confronting you and you have done your research, then you are mentally ready for business; ready to be your own boss. The next step is to become technically ready through your business plan.

Although never easy, millions before you have started their own businesses. Not all succeeded, but not all failed. When armed with research, months of pre-planning, a killer business plan and dedication the entrepreneur enters the world of business with a decided advantage. It is this advantage—early on that may be the difference between success and frustration, which can lead directly to failure. you will put this advantage to good use in the next chapter.

Chapter 4

Your First Business Plan

Writing a Winning Small Business Plan

Before every successful business launch, must come a business plan. And after every successful business launch, must come short and long-term plans. These are different from your initial business plan, though the two are related. In college, the keystone class in business school is usually a strategic planning course—and for good reason. Planning is the key to small business success.

It is necessary to plan, chart, and dream about the future of your business. (Without a vision, a business is blindfolded and will go round in circles until it finally collapses.) History is littered with blindfolded entities—businesses, people, countries—which had no direction, plan, or long-term goals to be met. One failed company, for example, was going to produce mail order material (tee-shirts, bumper stickers, posters, et al). However, instead of writing a complete business plan, only a skimpy one was produced and problem after problem followed. That approach broke a cardinal rule of business: Plan Ahead.

Your first business plan will be your blueprint for operations, financing, and growth. It will provide a guide to running and managing your company, as well as marketing your goods or services. The plan is an integral part in your quest for financing and capital, as it forecasts needed start-up and operating capital. As you project into the future, your anticipated growth patterns will be laid out, making goal setting easy for you in the future.

Before you write your plan, consider how important it will be to your start-up. Although the size of a plan may vary from a few pages to a few hundred, you need not worry about how big it is, just how thorough it is for your needs. We recommend you spend copious amounts of time refining this plan. After all, you may well present it to potential financial backers who are impressed by professionalism and thoroughness. Since this is the blueprint for your business, be sure to be realistic.

Do not be afraid to spend time brainstorming, researching, and writing the plan. You want the best plan, not the one that took ten minutes to write and looks like it.

Numerous books have been written on writing business plans, some of which contain actual examples. There are also computer software programs to help you create business plans. Chapter twelve lists some of each.

The following are basic areas you must know in order to prepare your business plan.

The Idea

You need a business idea. The more original the idea, the more close to it you will be and the harder you will work at it. Bill Gates and Donald Trump both love what they do and are good at it. That's not an accident—it is motivation and drive based on a passion for their businesses.

The simplest of entities—a small retail store—could mean the world for you, and that will make you work very hard to make it a success. You do not have to be IBM to be a "happy" business. But being unique and having a unique product can often bring about great success.

The Time Frame

The first step after picturing your business is to determine the time frame to start your company. It usually takes three to six weeks for incorporation certificates to be discussed, created, signed, sent to the state, and returned to the incorporator. It takes less time for other forms. And you should not conduct business until you are officially incorporated or documented with the state. So, from the time you decide to incorporate until the act is final is a minimum of about four weeks. You will need to take more time for your research, however.

Choosing a Name

You will also need to name your company. Remember, most states say the words "corporation", "incorporated," "inc", "company", "co", or "limited" must appear in the title of the corporation name. Limited partnerships usually must have "LP" or "Limited Partnership" in the name. The states regulate this, and it varies. Also, all business conducted with the company must include that title. For instance, if a person writes you a check, make sure it is made out *to the company* and includes the whole title. In addition, many states require that the name of the company be somehow identifiable with the owners. Assumed or fictitious names are used for companies, proprietors, or partnerships not wishing to identify the owners in the name of the company the customers deal with. Check your state for details. Some businesses are allowed to do business as (DBA) a different name than their company name. For most of you, this will not be a concern, but your state will have information on this.

Define Your Purpose and Goals

A vital step is to sit down and write out your purpose and first year goals. Your purpose should be clear and concise, yet it may not have to be so clear on the certificate of incorporation. Most companies are perpetual in duration.

And remember to ask a few very important questions (again, see chapter one) including: How much capital will we need? How much do we have? The answers to these questions will directly affect your company's operations, so answer them beforehand.

List Your Officers and Their Duties

For a corporation, you might have a list of officers for the board. Write those names down, along with the duties they will perform within the company. Most first businesses have a board of directors who are also stockholders and managers of the company.

Your Office and Agent

You will need an office and an agent, often called a Resident Agent if you go the corporation or limited liability company route. Whomever incorporates for you is usually the agent—often a lawyer, but not necessarily (it should simply be you)—and his or her address must be put on the document. The address of the company is usually an office, although it can be a home if you are zoned business or commercial. There are some businesses that can be run out of any home, though.

Plan Your Capital Requirements

Financially, you must realize that undercapitalization is a major problem of small businesses. Sources of capital are listed in chapter eight. You would do well to carefully think out and plan your capital needs before you create a business.

If you need $25,000 for your business, do not settle for $2500 and try and make due. It simply will not work. Wait until you can raise more money, and then try to use the money to leverage for a loan at a bank for the rest of the $25,000. By cutting short your capital infusion into your company, you may also cut short its life.

Determine Your Start-Up Equipment Needs

Equipment needs will vary, and you should shop around. If anything, that's the golden rule in frugal business management: shop around. Most medium-sized cities will have several business equipment sellers. Call ahead or get their catalogs and compare prices and quality, and then make the purchase. Another route, and a good one, is to get used equipment. Most cities auction off old municipal equipment from time to time, and that's a great place to pick up everything from desks to computers to filing cabinets. The federal government also has auctions and has a huge selection of items for sale, often at ridiculously low costs. See chapter twelve for information on other sources of equipment and supplies.

Location, Location, Location

Office space can be expensive, so once again, shop around. The beginner to business will most likely have to avoid central business districts and high-rent business office parks. However, smaller office parks and those located in suburbs or industrial parks are usually reasonable. Expect to pay from $5 to $20 a square foot in smaller cities like Fort Wayne, Indiana. In larger cities, expect to pay much more, up to $40 or more per square foot of prime office space in a major office building in Manhattan. Get enough space for your current needs and your future mid-term goals.

One possible way to obtain cheaper office space (and some government assistance) is to locate in an urban enterprise zone. While the terms may differ from city to city, the purpose does not. These zones are often located in older, inner-city areas, and their intention is to pump money back into the area in hopes of causing it to develop again. Often, the government will give tax breaks, grants, or other assistance to companies locating and hiring in these areas. It is certainly something to look into. Call your city's mayoral office or economic development office.

In addition, some cities have "incubators" or business development centers. These are usually full-service centers offering the beginning business receptionists, office space, conference rooms, equipment, etc. without the usual high costs. They are intended to aid new businesses in the initial stages of incorporation. The incubator can be of valuable assistance, especially if you have limited start-up and operating funds. Check your city government for one, or call the Chamber of Commerce for information.

Writing the Business Plan

A lot goes into a business plan. The things we discussed above as well as the results of your question and answer session, your goals and objectives, and your research will combine to create the plan.

You will pick and choose those parts of your research and plans that have a bearing on your operations and include them in the plan. Focus on the short-term in your plan, but plan for the long-term. That's, your plan is a blueprint to your first few years of operation, but it also forecasts future growth. This is done to preserve your sense of both short and long-term planning and to present potential investors with two things: your short-term operating goals and your long-term vision.

The plan should not be unrealistic. Leave your dreams out of it, but by all means include your goals. Just make sure they are obtainable and down to earth. Bankers, venture capitalists, and investors know impossible dreams when they see them and will pass you over if your goals are in the clouds.

A business plan has several parts to it. We have listed them below and include brief explanations on the purpose and importance of each section. For more in-depth analysis of a plan, check out one of the resources in chapter twelve.

Your business plan should include the following sections:

Cover Sheet
Introduction
Mission Statement
Overview of Your Business
Economic Analysis
Financial Analysis
Marketing Analysis
Summary
Indexes and Supporting Documents

Now we will discuss what goes into each part. Remember, your plan will vary depending on your size, goals and entity type. The key words here are thoroughness and realism. Be realistic when you write your plan. That's one reason it may take a month or a year to write it.

Cover Sheet. The cover sheet simply contains the name of your company, the principles, and the address and phone number. If you have a fax and/or an e-mail address, put them on it as well.

Introduction. This section is intended as a brief precursor to the plan that follows, the icebreaker so to speak. Try to state your general purpose in business and maybe an overview of your plan that follows. Keep it short, because you will have time to explain everything later.

Mission Statement. The mission statement of your plan should be your overall company philosophy and your company direction. It should identify the kind of business you will run and how you will be perceived by the public. Therefore, write a mission statement that reflects how *you would like the company to be if you were a customer*. Emphasize the uniqueness of your product, service, methods of doing business, commitment to quality and the customer, and your overall integrity.

Mission statements vary depending on the type of business, but all contain something on the values of the company, a description of the goods or services, and a statement of customer service objectives. Often they will contain information on relevant technologies and/or practices that make the company unique.

Overview of Your Business. This section will be written largely on the strength of your chapter one answers and your follow-up research. It is the broad description of your business, broken down into specific parts. Again, thoroughness will apply.

You will need to identify your start-up objectives, requirements, office location, personnel needs, and product/service identification and description.

List your short-term objectives, defining where you want to be in a year's time and how you plan to get there.

List your personnel requirements by planning how many employees you will need and what the skill level must be. You may need employees with skills you do not possess. A strength/weakness evaluation of your own skills will tell you what type of employees you need.

Include your management team. One way to do this is to create an organizational chart, listing managers and defining their functions. Pay attention to what strengths are needed in each management position. A SOHO business may have only one employee, that's fine. Just explain that.

Other items include a description of what product or service you are offering including how it is different or better.

Economic Analysis. Report on the state of the local, state, regional and national economy as it relates in general and specifically to your business and industry. Discuss such things as seasonal economic fluctuations visa-vis your company and how the economy will affect you. A discussion of your industry and internal and external effects on it is warranted here. List its growth trends, legal issues, strengths and weaknesses. Your part in this industry may be affected by the whole industry's health.

Financial Analysis. This is where the plan gets very technical. You will need to include all of the following in your plan. This part will help you project revenue and will give you a description of your financial state and future financial goals.

List your capital requirements and your start-up costs. Also, you want to list any sources of financing or capital you now have. A banker will be interested in how much money you have and are getting when he or she looks at a loan application.

Be accurate when estimating your projected sales figures. Stick to conservative figures. Support these projections with evidence and statistics.

Present a detailed cash flow section, listing the bi-weekly cash flow projections. Again, this will tie into your sales projections. This section may need to be extensive, especially if you want to show a potential investor your cash flow growth over a period of say six months to a year. The idea here is to show investors when cash will come into the business and at what rates. It will also give you an idea of your company's progress over the first year.

Another part is the one-year budget. This is your first year's operating budget including your fixed costs, overhead, salaries, taxes, advertising payments, lease payments, etc. Variable costs will be incurred after your start-up and may add or decrease your budgeted expenditures. When examining the revenue side of your budget, be conservative.

The next part is your balance sheet showing your net worth on a specific date. You will want to include a beginning balance sheet. List your assets (cash, receivables, prepaid expenses, etc.), liabilities (debts and accounts payable) and equity (stock values.)

Be sure to include a break even analysis that projects your expenses versus revenues in a projection that shows what sales will be needed to break even. You can also estimate profits with this analysis. You and your potential creditors will use this to see the feasibility of your business.

A final statement on your accounting methods and credit policy will round out this section. You may want to consider a professional accountant for thoroughness and professionalism. What kind of credit will you extend to your customers, and what will be your policies on bad debts, collections, and discounts?

Market Analysis. This section discusses your market, competition and methods of pricing, advertising, and selling. You need to discuss your competitors and the local market for your product/service. Discuss trends as well, and be sure to show how your product or service will be differentiated on price or quality and how you will use your uniqueness to generate sales. Include a complete section on marketing strategies and advertising. Another important part is to describe your distribution channels.

Summary. Simply wrap-up your plan with a few concluding remarks.

Indexes and Supporting Documents. Show any supporting documents, charts, or indexes you desire here. This is not a necessary part of the plan, but provides you with additional space for more information if needed.

This is a general overview of a business plan. More detailed books are written that flesh out the many things we discussed here. We recommend you purchase one or two of them.

As for the plan, we recommend a pause after you finish your initial business plan or proposal. This is a good way to get away from your ideas and to come back and look at them objectively. Wait two weeks and do not look at the plan or think about your business. Then re-read the plan, and get rid of any and all self-doubts you may still have.

You may decide to re-write your plan once you begin getting a cash flow and desire to obtain a loan. Many banks will not give loans to start-ups, but after they show cash flow, they may be more receptive. And as you expand and add employees or services and products, be sure to revise your plan to include them.

In fact, you may want to revise your plan periodically or to write another two to five year plan. This will contain many things, including your growth rates and goals after your first year of operation. chapter eleven has an entire section on strategic planning, the follow-up to writing a business plan.

Now that you have your plan, you can finally become your business. The next chapter deals with the many options available to potential businesspeople.

Your Business Options

The Seven Main Types of Business Structure

The modern small business starter has many options from which to choose a business entity. The entrepreneur may choose from simple forms like sole proprietors or complex ones like subchapter S-corporations. Each entity is designed for different business needs. Every type of business fits into one of the seven main entity types. Even SOHO businesses are covered by the choices of entity.

The options include sole proprietor, general partnership, limited partnership, corporation, s-corporation, limited liability company, and limited liability partnership. Additionally, all states have non-profit corporations and some have other forms of non-profit entities. Non-profit is usually for a charitable organization or a similar entity, and not usually in what we classify as a "business" that someone would be interested in starting. For information on these, contact a lawyer.

If your small business start-up involves buying an existing business, we suggest you hire or at least talk to a lawyer in addition to an accountant. The transactions are complicated and you will be glad you consulted them. Remember, too, that in buying a business, you are buying a "living, breathing" entity that's up and running already in other locations. This saves you some start-up concerns but also thrusts you into the business world right away.

We have provided a synopsis overview of each of the for-profit forms of business in order from simplest to most complex.

Additionally we have listed the pluses and minuses—the strengths and weaknesses—of each entity. These guides are generic in nature and intended to give you a general idea of what to expect with each type. Remember that in some states, certain business entities have certain rules or requirements that are unique to your state. To find out about your state, consult PART II and write to your state for further information.

The IRS defines a small business as a firm with annual gross receipts of $5 million or less for the past three years. That's most of you, and obviously you if you are just starting the business. With this in mind, choose your entity carefully to take advantage of tax, regulatory, legal, time, and finance considerations. Do not become the wrong business entity. Give it as much thought and consideration as you did your initial preparations.

To aid you in this, we have provided two worksheets at the back of this chapter. They will help you assess your specific business needs as they pertain to which entity to start. The first allows you to list pluses and minuses for each type. Place specific emphasis on listing pluses and minuses relating to your specific business. The second lists the factors influencing your decision. List your company's needs and check which business form best provides those needs. When you are done, use these sheets to compare and contrast the entity types and help you decide which best provides for your business needs.

The choice of entity election for your small business will depend on a variety of factors. These include your financial situation, technical needs, desired liability protection and goals. Some specific things to consider when selecting an entity type are:

1. **Liability Needs**
   How much protection from the company's actions do you personally require? Does your form of business generally require liability protection?

2. **Capital and Financial Requirements**
   How much capital do you have, and how much will you need over the next few years? How easily can you raise it under each of the entity types that follow?

3. **Size**
   How big are you now, and how big do you plan to become? What entity fits your business size?

4. **The Business You Are In**
   Certain businesses are best run under certain entity
   types. Does your business work best under a certain
   type?

5. **Scope of Your Business Operation**
   Are you doing business locally, statewide, or across
   state boundaries? What type of entity makes your
   business operation run best?

6. **Short and Long-Term Goals**
   What are your goals? How does each entity facilitate
   the fulfillment of those goals?

Again, much of your research and answered question material can
aid you in determining which type of business entity to elect. Keep in
mind the six factors above. Read up on each of these types of business
structures, and decide which one is right for your small business. Then
use the attached worksheets to help you make your election.

Sole Proprietorship

This is the simplest and most common form of business in America.
There are an estimated sixteen million sole proprietors in the United
States, and the number grows every year, especially with the surge
in SOHO businesses. A sole proprietorship is not a legal entity like a
corporation or limited liability company. This is because the sole
proprietor needs neither complex liability protection nor state licensing in order to operate. At most, a sole proprietor might need a
local business license and must follow some withholding
requirements.

Operating a sole proprietorship removes many of the
burdensome government regulations from day-to-day considerations.
Usually, the most intrusive thing is your yearly income taxes. It is you
against the world but not against a Goliath of government red tape.
However, you must abide by any regulations that do affect you, so be
aware of them.

Many small businesses and home office businesses are sole
proprietors because they do not yet need the protection afforded by
incorporation or are too small to efficiently become a corporation.

Sometimes they are sole proprietors because their goals are simple, thus eliminating the need to consider the effects of taxes or liability protection. Those with limited funds and limited goals (at least initially) may choose to become a sole proprietor first. Incorporation or partnership can wait until the company expands.

That's not to say all SOHO or micro businesses are sole proprietors. If you need the liability protection, go with the corporation, the limited partnership, or the limited liability company.

We have listed some of the pluses and minuses of this simple yet effective business entity. You may come up with more relative to your business situation.

Pluses

- You get all the profits.
- Easy to start: less paperwork to start it up and keep it running. (You avoid lawyers, too!)
- Income is taxed just once as personal income, thus eliminating complex tax forms.
- Low start-up cost and often low operating costs.
- You are the boss!
- Many sole proprietors can operate their business from home.
- Great for part-time businesses and SOHO businesses.

Minuses

- You are personally liable for all business debts.
- You have unlimited legal liability.
- All decisions and much of the work are on your shoulders, at least initially.
- Growth and financial opportunities are limited.
- It might be more expensive for things like health insurance.
- You are limited in the amount of capital you will be able to receive.
- The business ceases upon the death of the proprietor.

In most states, becoming a sole proprietor is very easy. For example, in Indiana, a sole proprietor needs only register with the County Recorder's office. Of course, there may be zoning requirements and some other considerations such as withholding and sales tax identification numbers, Federal employer Identification Number, and local and state regulations to follow. But on the whole, the sole proprietor is an excellent choice for the certain SOHO, part-time, and/or micro businesses.

If your needs and goals are simple, this is the way to start your business.

General Partnerships

This is where two or more people create a for-profit, unincorporated business and are all part owners of it. In some ways, the general partnerships is like a dual or multi-person sole proprietorship. Certainly the usual requirements and rules governing each are somewhat similar.

Under a general partnership, both partners are equal partners in the venture and share the duties, responsibilities, revenue, and liabilities equally. Partnerships are affected by creating a partnership agreement, which is a simple contract between two or more people. It contains certain information that clarifies what the partnership is about: the partners, the responsibilities of each, the duration, the management, and financial arrangements.

Pluses

- Simple to start.
- Like the sole proprietor, income is taxed as personal income.
- Little regulation and start-up requirements.
- Good for simple businesses or short-term business situations.
- Potentially unlimited duration.
- It may be easier to raise capital in a partnership than a sole proprietor.

Minuses

- No liability protection for the partners.
- The partners may eventually end up doing unequal amounts of work.
- Partnerships can lead to personal troubles between the partners.
- Actions of one partner bind all partners to it.
- If you need large amounts of capital or large businesses, you may want to become a corporation instead.
- Partnership ends when one owner dies or leaves the company.

Limited Partnerships

The limited partnership is one in which there are two types of partners: general, who assumes all responsibilities as owner and manager; and limited, who is limited in his or her liability to the amount he or she invested in the business. This form of business is affected in the same way as a general partnership, with one exception. The limited partnership is often required to register with the state government. Usually a form is filled out and sent to the state for approval.

A partnership might choose to become a limited partnership depending on certain factors. Foremost would be the desire of one partner to supply capital and not effort. That would be the limited partner. The remaining general partner(s) would be responsible for day-to-day operations and would assume the partnership's liability. If you do not wish to become a corporation or limited liability company but need to protect the liability of your investing partners, this is for you.

Limited partnerships have more regulations and usually require state licensing, which sets them apart from general partnerships. Consult PART II for your state's limited partnership requirements.

Pluses

- The limited partners have liability protection.
- Income is taxed as personal income only.

- Potentially unlimited duration.
- Good way to raise capital through limited partners.
- Little government regulation.

Minuses

- The general partners have no liability protection and do all of the work.
- The partnership ends when one partner dies or leaves the company.
- More state start-up requirements and regulations.
- Limited partner can take his or her investment out of the company.
- Limited partner may become disgruntled if the business is not run well.

Limited Liability Company

The limited liability companies are newer business entities that are hybrids of limited partnerships and corporations and provide the best features of both, such as ease of formation, tax savings, and liability protection. These are fast becoming a very popular business election.

The limited liability corporation, or LLC, is basically a company with corporate liability protection and stockholding capabilities and the tax advantages of a partnership or sole proprietor. The income of a limited liability company is taxed at the shareholder or owner level, thus eliminating the double taxation that occurs with corporations. However, the liability protection affords it the shelter many small business owners desire.

Recent laws have enabled LLC's to obtain almost the same liability and tax protections as S-corporations, without certain corporation requirements and regulations. For small businesses that desire most of the benefits of incorporation this is the way to go. An S-corp, mentioned below, is similar in function but more restrictive. You really have to look at your needs in order to choose between the two. Here is where an accountant or a lawyer can come in handy.

Pluses

- Income is taxed once.
- Can have more than one class of stock.

- Have unlimited liability protection like corporations.
- New laws enable this election to be basically a corporation with great tax benefits and stock regulations.

Minuses

- Still not a corporation with the credibility offered by the "Inc." at the end of the business name.
- May have a limited, rather than unlimited, life span. Usually a set number of years, determined by state.
- This can be a tricky election.
- May be under more IRS scrutiny.

Becoming a limited liability company usually requires filing certain forms, much on the lines of a corporation. However, it can usually be done easily. Be sure to study your particular state's requirements before making the election.

Limited Liability Partnership

This is very similar to the LLC listed above. The difference is that it is a partnership with protection being afforded to the partners as one. As such is does not offer the incentive of raising capital through stock. you will probably not use this election, but if you do a section is listed in the next chapter on how to do it. A plus/minus section is not listed here. See the LLC plus/minus section for a similar list.

Corporation (C-Corp)

This is a for-profit organization created under the auspices of your state government. It is incorporated to do business within your state by an act of your state government. Millions of corporations dot the business landscape.

A corporation is owned by one or more people called stockholders, but those stockholders are separate from the company itself. That's to say, they, as stockholders, have unlimited liability protection from the actions of the corporation. They cannot be held responsible for the actions of the corporation. That onus falls upon the company executives and the company itself. Be aware of this fact before you make any decisions. The corporation offers legal protection for its owners, as they are separated from the company. This can be a consideration for those needing extra liability protection.

Because it is licensed to operate by state charter, the corporation is more regulated than most other forms of business entity. Start-up requirements usually include forms, fees, and stock certificates. However, the corporation offers distinct advantages, including better capital generation, stock, liability protection, unlimited life, and a professional name. And because of state recognition the corporate "Inc." at the end of a name may be a psychological aid in company credibility. Many companies are incorporated in certain states for tax, regulation, and financial reasons. Two popular states for this are Nevada and Delaware. you will probably want to just stick with your own state.

Here are some strengths and weaknesses of this election form.

Pluses

- Unlimited liability protection for stockholders.
- Can offer more than one class of stock.
- The "Inc." name may add credibility and professionalism to your business name.
- Ability to grow is enhanced.
- Raising capital is easier than some other forms such as sole proprietorships.
- Hierarchy and structure may make duties within the corporation easier to define for partners starting a business.

Minuses

- Income is taxed at corporate and stockholder level.
- Many on-going state regulations and yearly requirements.
- To do business in another state, you must file foreign corporation registrations with that state.
- Company subjected to desires of a board of directors representing the stockholders.
- Start-up is more lengthy and expensive than other elections.

The election is accomplished by filing certain forms with your Secretary of State. Additionally, yearly or bi-yearly requirements include such things as annual reports. Your state requirements will vary.

Most large companies are corporations primarily for the liability protection. You will make your election depending on your needs. However, you will want to at least investigate limited liability companies and S-corporations before making the regular corporation election. Either of the former will probably save you a great deal in tax savings.

Sub-Chapter S-Corporation (S-Corp)

A special form of the corporation that you might try is the sub-chapter "S" corporation. This was created to give the owners of the corporation all the benefits (including limited liability) of the regular corporation but without high corporate taxes. In some way, the limited liability company does a similar thing. S-corp income is reported on the owners' income taxes, thus reducing the amount of taxes paid and theoretically increasing profit.

An S-corp is a stock corporation licensed by a state as a corporation and classified by the IRS as a sub-chapter "S" corporation. This election is made by filing form 2553 with the IRS. The S-corp can have seventy-five or fewer American stockholders holding one class of stock. It allows for transfer of stock to family members and includes the prime incentive of single taxation on all company income.

Many businesses choose either the S-corp or the newer limited liability company when electing a business type. Ongoing changes in tax and regulatory laws affect all business entities, especially S-corps and limited liability companies. Keep abreast of current rules and regulations. They may have changed since publication.

Pluses

- Stockholders have liability protection for actions of company.
- Income is taxed only once.

- Growth and capital raising is easier than certain other entity types.
- Losses can be used to offset personal income.
- Is basically a corporation but with better tax structure.

Minuses

- Has only one class of stock.
- Has many start-up requirements, including more Federal requirements and potential state requirements.
- May be under more IRS scrutiny.
- Must adhere to strict fiscal guidelines.
- Can only form one every five years.

If you incorporate, you are a business of the state in which you incorporate. If you need to set up a store or do business in another state, that state will recognize you as a *foreign corporation*. That's, you are foreign to that state. Many states require incorporated businesses from other states to file forms in order to do business in that state. If you need to do business in another state, have your lawyer check the other state's laws first, and file any applicable forms. You can do this yourself, but you may want to get a lawyer to make sure all the requirements are met.

These business entity types will no doubt change over the course of the years to come, but for now, they are the main types. Remember to carefully consider your election. This will affect your company for the next several years. Later, you can always become a different business entity, but you must check the rules and regulations before you do so.

Worksheet: Business Type Analysis

	Plus	Minus
Sole Proprietor	1. 2. 3. 4. 5.	1. 2. 3. 4. 5.
General Partnership	1. 2. 3. 4. 5.	1. 2. 3. 4. 5.
Limited Partnership	1. 2. 3. 4. 5.	1. 2. 3. 4. 5.
Limited Liability Company	1. 2. 3. 4. 5.	1. 2. 3. 4. 5.
Limited Liability Partnership	1. 2. 3. 4. 5.	1. 2. 3. 4. 5.
Incorporation	1. 2. 3. 4. 5.	1. 2. 3. 4. 5.
Other	1. 2. 3. 4. 5.	1. 2. 3. 4. 5.

Worksheet: Business Type Election

Keep in mind your requirements will be based on: Liability Needs, Capital and Finances, Size, Business You Are In, Scope of Your Business Operation, Short and Long-Term Goals. Fill out this sheet according to what is necessary for your business. Check off those entities that provide what you need.

Business Entity Types

Requirements	1	2	3	4	5	6	7
1._____	☐	☐	☐	☐	☐	☐	☐
2._____	☐	☐	☐	☐	☐	☐	☐
3._____	☐	☐	☐	☐	☐	☐	☐
4._____	☐	☐	☐	☐	☐	☐	☐
5._____	☐	☐	☐	☐	☐	☐	☐
6._____	☐	☐	☐	☐	☐	☐	☐
7._____	☐	☐	☐	☐	☐	☐	☐
8._____	☐	☐	☐	☐	☐	☐	☐
9._____	☐	☐	☐	☐	☐	☐	☐
10._____	☐	☐	☐	☐	☐	☐	☐
11._____	☐	☐	☐	☐	☐	☐	☐
12._____	☐	☐	☐	☐	☐	☐	☐
13._____	☐	☐	☐	☐	☐	☐	☐
14._____	☐	☐	☐	☐	☐	☐	☐
15._____	☐	☐	☐	☐	☐	☐	☐

1=Sole Proprietor 2=General Partnership 3=Limited Partnership 4=Limited Liability Company 5=Limited Liability Partnership 6=Corporation 7=S-Corporation

How Do I Do This?

The Basics of Forming Each Type of Business Entity

By now you should know how you want to structure your company. In other words, what business entity will you elect to become. Your questions have been answered, and your plan has been written. Now you can begin the process of actually starting a business. At this stage, you will be a few days or weeks away from actually being in business. Therefore, you want to make sure you are ready to enter into business. That's, is everything in order, and are you finally prepared to begin the actual work of your small business? If you are doing it part-time are, you ready for the extra hours (which you have been putting into doing your plan anyway)? If this is a full-time venture, make sure you have tied up any and all loose ends with your old job and that you have enough financial resources to last you through the start-up. The operative word here is preparedness. If you have been diligent, you are ready.

Remember that you can get help from accountants, lawyers, and others if you are still unsure about which entity to start.

Each type of entity requires different processes, forms, fees, and regulations. Each takes different durations of time to form. Each has different ongoing requirements from either the states or federal governments. But basically, each is fairly easy to start. This chapter will examine the requirements for each and just what it is like to go through the process.

For entities like corporations, partnerships, and limited liability companies, the requirements vary state-by-state. Some states have more requirements than others and charge more in the way of fees and taxes. By requesting and then reading literature from your Secretary of State, you can better decide—with your lawyer, accountant, partner, SCORE officer, and/or your work from this book—what would be the best entity for you.

While many people use lawyers to incorporate, you may do it yourself. Also, a number of resources exist in the form of private companies and publications that show you how to incorporate yourself. Several are listed in chapter twelve.

When starting a business, never go with the cheapest and easiest route simply for those reasons. If you need the legal protection of a limited liability company or even that of a corporation, go that route. Likewise, if you are starting a simple SOHO, you may be able to get away with being a sole proprietor or general partnership. Depending on your needs, you will enter into whatever form best suits your business. Our last advice here is again to be thorough in your selection process.

The following start-up tips are for all business starters at start-up and after. They are intended to save you money or time. Glance through to see which apply to you.

1. You will most likely need to file Form SS-4 Federal Employer Identification Number with the IRS. This can be done while you are forming your company. A sole proprietor may not need one of these. Consult the IRS for further information.
2. Consult an accountant and get advice on tax rules and filing information. A CPA working for himself or herself is often a good bet, because the service is more personal, and if he or she has a CPA, more professional.
3. Prepare your data in advance so it is handy for the lawyer. Include all relevant data including company name and address, your name and address, the number and type of shares available, the purpose of the business, and the duration (usually perpetual). Use our worksheet "Vital Start-Up Information" in appendix C to do this.

4. You can save money by calling several lawyers to obtain a "best price". Be sure to have the lawyer spell out exactly what services that includes. Or call the Bar Association's Lawyer Referral service. In a city like Fort Wayne, it costs about $15. It will vary.

5. You can save on W-2 forms and the like by getting them directly from the IRS. Although they will probably give you only half a dozen, many small businesses do not need more than that, at least for the first year. After that, buy them in bulk at an office supply store.

6. Attend business workshops, seminars, and expositions in your area or state on a regular basis before and after start-up. They can be invaluable for discovering business information, products, suppliers, and people.

7. Continuing education classes for adults at local, state, or community colleges or at technical schools can help you, partners, or employees learn current practices or brush up on past knowledge. Often, you do not need a previous college degree to attend.

8. Always keep records for at least five to eight years and keep your start-up records forever. We suggest, however, keeping all of your records *permanently*. Most small businesses will be able to find the space for the records, although every few years you may want to cull records you do not need.

9. You can always start as a sole proprietor or partnership and then incorporate as you get larger or your needs change.

10. For that professional look, no matter what business you start, use letterhead, business cards, and professional appearance in your business dealings. Disorganization turns off customers and investors.

11. Check with local authorities for licenses and zoning information.

With that said, let's examine how to start each of the seven entity types.

Sole Proprietor

All you need to do is become the business. You do not need to fill out any "legal" forms of incorporation. There is no sole proprietor equivalent to the Articles of Incorporation or General Partnership Articles. However, there are certain state and local licensing documents and forms that must be completed. Obtain these at your county recorder's office. Usually this will be a business license. Other licenses may be required from your state for certain business activities. You should contact the state to inquire about required state forms and/or professional or other licenses. Tax forms may need to be filed for withholding and sales tax. Again, you will know if you need to file those.

We suggest that you go through the eight step process just as you would for a partnership or corporation. In fact, you will need to in order to complete your business plan and to set up the financial arrangement for your business. You probably will need a sales tax identification number for retail and employer identification number as well.

Once you have set up your business, you can get an account at a bank for checking and other activities. Some very small businesses can simply use their own checking, but we advise looking into a separate checking account.

One final note. For most, including many SOHO businesses, this is the way to go, but think about it first. Remember you have all liability on your shoulders, including financial and legal. Still, this is the easiest and best route for most of you. You can always incorporate later, as your company grows.

General Partnership

Like the sole proprietor, the general partnership is easy to enter into. Once again, you simply become the partnership. You and your partner will be general partners, each assuming a share of the risk and return and a share of the duties.

An oral agreement is all that's *needed*, but a written agreement is practical and smart. This way, you and your partner both agree to exactly the same terms and your signatures make it a contract. Be as concise and exact as possible, as a safeguard against possible problems later on. Include the partnership name, the partners, the responsibilities of each, the duration, the management, and financial arrangements, as well as any special sections you feel are necessary. Include complete details about each partner's duties and responsibilities. You might want to bullet them to make them stand out on the agreement. Have the agreement signatures notarized, and each person should keep an original copy of the instrument.

If you have any questions, talk with a lawyer about what to put into the agreement. Still, this is a basic form of business, and you should not have to see a lawyer. Just be concise and thorough in your partnership agreement.

Once you have your partnership agreement, file for a business license with your county recorder's office. Make sure you have any and all licenses needed. Check your local and state governments for these.

After this, you may set up your checking account at a local bank. It is prudent to leave the finances to one of the partner, and this should be noted as part of the partnership agreement. However, both should be able to utilize checking accounts.

A periodic review of your partnership agreement and your business plan will ensure that your partnership is on the right track.

Limited Partnership

The limited partnership starts the more complex start-up entities, although the processes are all very easy. Here, you have one or more general partners and one or more limited partners. States regulate limited partnerships more closely than general partnerships or sole proprietors. Thus, it is a good idea to contact your state for more information (forms, rules, codes) before talking to a lawyer.

To form a limited partnership, formulate and write a partnership agreement that clearly enumerates the same things for a general partnership as we listed in the section above and the role in the partnership of the limited partner(s).

Most states will require you to file a form called a limited partnership certificate or a certificate of limited partnership. Get this from a lawyer or the state, file it with the appropriate fee, and wait for the return certificate. Some states may require your partnership agreement be submitted with their forms. If so, simply comply.

Next, you will generally file for a business license at your county recorder's or clerk's office and apply for any other necessary state licenses. After this, you may set up your checking account at a local bank. Again, it is prudent to leave the finances to one of the partners, and this should be noted as part of the partnership agreement.

A periodic review of your partnership agreement and your business plan will ensure that your partnership is on the right track.

Limited Liability Company

The limited liability company is set up in similar fashion as the corporation.

Once ready, simply set up your structure of partners, investors, and officers. File the certificate of limited liability organization (name may vary), consent (certificate) of registered agent, and any trade name registration needed. These are filed at your Secretary of State. Others may be necessary, depending on your state requirements.

The fees vary by state but are generally not too expensive. In Indiana, it costs about $110 to start up an LLC, and the fees will be higher or lower depending on your state's fees and requirements. Some states do not have a form per se but will provide a list of guidelines for inclusion in the articles of organization. Usually you will put the name of the company, the address, the name and address of the registered agent, the date the company is to dissolve, the names of the organizers or managers, and rights the company will have. This is a vague template that your state may or may not follow. It is signed by the organizers and dated. The words limited liability company or LLC or L.L.C. must usually be included in your company name.

When you write your state for forms, you will be given a list of fees and forms to file. Once these forms are submitted you will receive a certification and can get your bank account, and your business license at your county recorder's office. Again, be sure to check with your state or lawyer for any other licenses particular to your business or industry.

Limited Liability Partnership

The limited liability partnership is similar to the LLC except it is a partnership. Where it exists, this entity is elected by filing the limited liability partnership certificate or selection. Again, this may not be a form, and you may have to create it yourself. Not all states have this election, so write to your state for more information. LLP or Limited Liability Partnership must generally appear in the name.

After you start it, though, you can get your bank account, your county business license, and any other licenses.

Corporation

Incorporating is similar in process to forming a limited liability company, except most states have a simple one or two page form that you must fill out and submit. You can, under most circumstances, write your own articles if you wish to include more information than is included on the form. For most of you, the form that comes from the state will be enough. Most states have separate forms for regular and professional corporations.

Usually, your state form will ask you for the name of the corporation; the incorporators; the registered agent; the initial number of stock shares, their value and type; your duration (usually forever); the original company officers; and the purpose of your incorporation (what are you going to do).

Generally, if you are doing this yourself, you will first reserve a trade name, register your agent, and file the articles of incorporation. The state will return the forms as filed, and you may start business. You will need a corporate minutes book with stock certificates showing your initial shares and the value—use simple forms or go to an office stationery store for these. A shareholder's meeting must be held after you incorporate to elect officers of your board. That board must then meet for the first time to select bylaws. Since it is your company, you will most likely have the minutes and stock shares, so your first meeting should be quite easy. Remember to document the meeting though, you are now a business and should conduct affairs accordingly.

These are generalized guidelines but are usually true for most states. Write your state for complete requirements.

If you are using an attorney to incorporate, he or she will do all of this. Your signatures will be required on many of the forms. If more information is needed, your lawyer may write an articles of incorporation to include much more information that's pertinent to your wishes and your company's goals. The attorney will handle most of the requirements for you, *but make sure in writing what services he or she will perform for what fee.* The minimum is filing for a reserved name, filing your articles of incorporation, getting stock certificates, creating bylaws, and filing your Federal Identification Numbers. Simply ask the attorney what the fee encompasses.

Either way, you fill out, sign, and send your incorporation forms to the state.

You will also write your bylaws as mentioned above. These are the codes, rules, and regulations that are used in the day-to-day operation of the company—*no matter the size.* They can be as complex as you wish, however, they should cover most contingencies that *could* affect your company. Often a lawyer can do this for you in lieu of an initial stockholders meeting or can assist you. Operating under standard business codes, the requirements are straightforward and designed to keep your business running in a professional manner in compliance with laws and codes. These bylaws must be registered with the Secretary of State.

S-Corporation

For a sub-chapter "S" corporation, you will file your forms as described above. Some states may have slightly different forms. Generally, the only real difference is that you or your lawyer must file IRS Form 2553—Election by a Small Business Corporation—with the Internal Revenue Service. This states your legal right to become an S-corporation. After this, your only differences come in the number of stockholders and the annual tax returns. The S-corp will be required to file income tax returns for S-corporations. However, all income will be taxed at the shareholder level.

These are outlines of the typical start-up requirements for most states. States vary, though, so read your state's guidelines in the back of this book, and write your state for more information.

Special Notes for Start-Up Businesses

- The address for the company can be your home if you follow zoning and IRS codes. Your home office should not be a place where customers come, unless you are zoned for business as well as residential.
- Any additional local or special state fees may also be required with regulatory licenses. To incorporate, a lawyer will cost between $400-$1000. Usually it is around $500. Tax number fees can cost more, as can other fees (incorporation and limited partnership and stock fees).
- Self-incorporation forms can be obtained in a variety of paperback booklets and kits available at most nation-wide chain bookstores or even business stationery stores. Check your local bookstores.
- Copies of the Indiana Incorporation Form and State Sales Tax Number/Withholding Number form are shown below. They will vary in content and length from state to state. In addition, we have listed rules, fees, forms needed, and regulations for all fifty states and the District of Columbia in PART II. This gives more details on your particular state.
- Remember that you are required to hold a Board of Director's meeting at least annually and to submit annual or biennial reports if you are a corporation or limited liability company. Again, know your state's requirements.
- For certain larger start-ups, avoiding lawyers will be extremely difficult for most people. They do, after all, handle incorporations all the time and will answer your questions. Most novice incorporators have dozens of questions, and the lawyer should be patient with you and answer them.

Chapter 7

Franchising

The Other Alternative

At this point, we feel it might be worthwhile to tell you about franchising, since some of you might be interested in it. Some of you will buy franchises, and some of you may eventually franchise your business as it grows and becomes successful.

Franchising is a business concept whereby a parent company uses affiliated owners to distribute or sell its products or services. It usually involves the parent company collecting an up-front licensing fee, an annual fee, and a percentage of the profit from the franchisee. In return, the franchisee gets to use the company name, product/service, and participate in the collective advertising of the whole firm. Some franchises have more leeway in day-to-day operations and even in planning than others. It all depends on the franchiser and its business practices.

Starting-up a franchise business can run the gamut from modest to costly. Some can be had for a few thousand dollars, but these are typically not location franchises but rather business ideas and systems you run from your home or through mail order. Others are more involved, some costing several hundred thousand dollars to start. Many franchises work out deals with potential franchisees in order to finance the purchase of the franchise. The fees and costs to operate a franchise also vary greatly.

This small business opportunity is a fast-growing segment of the American small business economy. In essence, owning a franchise is like owning a small business that's part of a big business. For instance, if you own one Subway franchise, you run it like a small business but are actually part of a giant network of other franchise locations and the corporate headquarters.

The Franchise Opportunities Handbook—published by the Department of Commerce—reports that franchising is equal to 33% of U.S. retail sales. The restaurant business is increasingly franchise-driven, which means more competition for local restaurants. What this means, of course, is that franchising as a whole is big business with a small business feel. With more and more products and services offered under the guise of franchises, it makes sense to talk about them in a small business book.

Everyone knows and uses franchised businesses. Some of them include Pack 'N' Mail mailing centers, The Glass Mechanix window repair system, car rental's Rent-A-Wreck, the copy center Sir Speedy Printer Center, fast food giants like McDonalds and Pizza Hut, and auto repair/painters Midas and Maaco. Scores of other established and commonplace franchises operate across the nation, even in small towns and rural areas. Many small business publications have information and sometimes rankings of the best franchises. There is ample opportunity for the potential franchiser in this growing market segment if he or she has what it takes (and that includes money and determination.)

This may be an option for you if you are unsure about going it "alone" in business. But be aware that this is no easier a route than any of the other options. It takes long hours, a lot of money, and determination for the franchise to succeed. The only difference is the fact that the franchiser is behind you, which may eliminate some of the anxiety and uncertainty associated with starting a business. Some pluses and minuses are:

Pluses

- Combined advertising for the whole chain
- You start with everything: product/service, training, name recognition, and brands

- You are part of an established, most likely successful, business network
- The company often provides technical advice and management training programs

Minuses

- Can have a high start-up cost
- The legal and regulatory requirements are tremendous at start-up
- A franchise puts pressure on you to perform well for yourself *and* the parent company
- You are not a truly independent business; you might have to follow parent company's pricing and product policies
- Can be expensive to run in terms of fees and percentages given to parent company

Small office or home office franchises exist, and their ads can be found in many small business magazines. Typically, these will be low-cost, less profitable franchises. The franchiser may not be able to provide as much technical assistance and marketing prowess as the larger franchises. However, you may be able to start one part-time and then move to full-time. But be wary of anything that sounds too good to be true, especially if you go looking for a part-time SOHO franchise.

With that said, when you look at a franchise, the franchiser—the company that licenses its product to you—should be willing to provide you with the following types of assistance at start-up and during the life of the franchise. These items should be clearly enumerated in the prospectus and in any contracts you sign.

1. Location analysis and counsel
2. Store development aid, including lease negotiation
3. Store design and equipment purchasing
4. Initial employee and management training, and continuing management counseling
5. Advertising and merchandising counsel and assistance
6. Standardized procedures and operations

7. Centralized purchasing with consequent savings
8. Financial assistance in the establishment of the business
   (Source: *Franchise Opportunities Handbook*)

None of these is guaranteed however. You must carefully analyze prospective franchises by reading the literature they send you and by asking questions of claims and statistics. If a franchiser does not supply you with everything the government publications recommend, ask for the missing information. This is one case where the government is on your side, Also, get everything in writing. Remember, this is your future, so take the time to think it out.

When you begin contemplating a franchise, the Department of Commerce recommends the following in order to evaluate the risk and returns of franchising. This list is a good general guide. Again, other publications and books will have more detailed information, and we urge you to consult them.

- **Be Aware of the Risks**—Like any business, there are good franchises and bad franchises. Take the time to find out which is which.
- **Protect Yourself by Self-Evaluation**—Again, ask yourself whether you can handle the strains—financial, physical, mental—before you franchise.
- **Protect Yourself by Investigating the Franchise**—Compare and contrast; talk to a variety of franchisers and franchisees.
- **Protect Yourself by Studying Disclosure Statements**—Here, the company should provide you with prospectuses or disclosure statements that contain information of several details of the franchise. *Ask for one if they do not give you one.* This is important.
- **Protect Yourself by Checking Out the Disclosures**—Field check the information in the disclosures by calling or visiting franchisees.
- **Question Earnings Claims**—Some states force franchisers to provide detailed information on this, some do not. This is the whole point of the business, so be careful.

- **Obtain Professional Advice**—This can be from government, industry, or individuals. The only thing that matters is that you do it. Talk to franchisers, franchisees, bankers, business leaders, lawyers, and accountants, just as for any other business option.
- **As a Potential Franchisee, Know Your Legal Rights**—Discuss this with a lawyer, and consult the Franchise Opportunities Handbook, which is available from the U.S. Government Printing Office and other government resources.

In addition to the Commerce Department's handbook, several organizations and sources of information are available to the potential franchisee. Another government source is the Federal Trade Commission's guide to buying a franchise. It is a complete guide to the do's and don'ts. Also, your state government may regulate the sale of franchises, so you might want to investigate your state. The SBA may be able to help with some of its publications and with SCORE advice.

The *USA Today* newspaper runs an Investment Opportunities page in the Money section every Wednesday. This contains companies advertising in the following areas: Franchises, Business Opportunities, Investment Properties, Business Marketplace, and Auctions. Several franchises are listed, from car painters and fast food to tax preparation services and sports shops. This is a good place to start looking for opportunities.

Two organizations that aid franchisees are the American Association of Franchisees and Dealers, and the International Franchise Association. These organizations can provide assistance, benefits, and networking opportunities. Many small business magazines like *Nation's Business, Income Opportunities,* and *Entrepreneur* devote copious space monthly to franchises and franchise news.

The addresses, phone numbers, and/or Internet addresses of many of these sources of information on franchising may be found in chapter twelve. Also, do not forget to talk to anyone you know who has purchased a franchise before. He or she will be able to tell you the ups and downs, as well as the road blocks and pitfalls to be aware of.

Buying a franchise begins with the eight Department of Commerce recommendations listed above. Do them *with* a lawyer so that you are *100 percent sure of each and every detail*. Evaluate the market, yourself, the franchise, its claims, and the franchiser's representatives. Prepare your own business plan based on the one in this book, and be sure to ask yourself every conceivable question before entering into a franchise agreement. The plan will help you evaluate your goals, as well as prepare you for your new business.

The next step is to obtain the necessary financing and documentation to start the franchise. The documents vary as do the capital requirements. Again, you will need a lawyer to go over the documents, which vary from franchise to franchise. It is important to remember not to rush into anything. Be sure of all the legal, accounting, tax, financial, and personal responsibilities you will have to yourself, the franchise store, and the parent company.

Franchising can be a wonderful, fulfilling career. It can lead to other businesses. If you are not purchasing one, you might think about franchising your small business some day. It can also be financially successful for you, if you work at it. Just know the facts first.

Chapter 8

Money: The Root of All Business

Finding, Raising, and Begging for Business Capital

Money is the root of all business. This is not a catchy phrase designed to get your attention. You have bought this book, so we have your attention. Rather, this is the blunt truth. No matter what your other motivations, making money has to rank near the top of your small business "reasons to start a business" list. And the old adage that "it takes money to make money" is true enough.

With all the cliches out of the way, start-up capital is one of the most vital parts of your start-up. In order to properly start and run your business, you will need some amount of capital. The amount depends on your needs and your goals. Your business plan will contain this information. It is vital to properly capitalize your small business and to develop resources and methods to obtain further capital. A company without proper financing will have a tough time competing with established competitors. Additionally, this will raise the risk of your business eventually closing or going bankrupt; neither of which you want.

This chapter will examine the many resources available to you in this quest. Other resources will be available in your local community or your state, so check around.

Capital is basically money used to run your business. When you start your business, chances are your first source of capital will probably be your own wallet, savings account, or cashed-in insurance policy—something along those lines. Using your own savings is the simplest way to get start-up capital. You are the first (and maybe only) person to be interested in investing in this company you are founding. Therefore you must be prepared to shell out your own hard-earned savings to help your business through its first few months, realizing that you could lose your money. If you are working part-time in your business, you may have income from your regular job and that can also be used for the company.

Many other sources of start-up capital exist. These include selling stock, loans, friends, partners, and venture capitalists. Let's examine a more complete listing.

Sources of Capital/Financing

Stock

Selling stock can bring capital to your company in the form of shareholder's equity. Stock is an issuance of ownership in a company. It is usually affected by a sale of a certificate for money to an individual or organization. When you start a corporation you will have a certain number of shares issued at start-up. This might be all the capital you need. However, if you need more, you may have to make a *public offering*. This is where you go through an investment banker or brokerage to sell your stock to the public. This usually involves state and federal regulations, so in order to do it, you should talk to a *qualified* accountant, lawyer, or banker. This can also be a costly route if you consider fees and percentage fees. Still, it is a viable and commonplace way to raise capital.

Another way is to do a *direct public offering* (DPO). This is a stock offering that you offer "on your own" to the public, without many of the associated banker/broker fees. Each state regulates this in different ways, so write to your state for information. If you receive approval from your state securities commission, you will be allowed to offer a set amount of DPO stock to the pubic. Most states will insist you set your stock price at $5 per share. Types of DPOs include:SCOR— Small Corporate Offering Registration—which can raise up to $1,000,000; Regulation-A, under which you can sell up $5,000,000 in stock; and SB-2 offerings, which can raise up to $10,000,000. You will want to research these further with the help of a securities lawyer or an accountant. You will probably need them to assist you in filing as well.

Many investors will be wary of a start-up business, which is why you might have to wait until your company is making a steady cash flow and is growing before offering a DPO. And if you do not raise a minimum of the projected funds in a year, you must refund the money to investors. It boils down to risk and return.

Venture Capitalist

A venture capitalist is an individual or organization that invests in companies deemed worthy of growth and profitability. Steve Jobs got his start-up capital for the original Apple Computers from a venture capitalist. Typically venture capital firms will invest in a certain sized company, usually one out of its start-up phase and well into its product's or service's expanding growth phase. The potential of rapid market growth for your company is the main criteria to receive capital from one of these sources.

Venture capitalists are professionals and not easily won over. In order to attract one and to sell your company's prospects you have to be professional yourself. A venture capitalist will want to see your plan and your financials (balance sheets, cash flow statements, etc.), along with meeting with you. The capitalist will determine whether your company has a past record of success that will bring about a future record of growth. If your company fits this profile, you might attract a venture capitalist.

Few start-ups will be financed this way, so the best route is to start your business, grow, and then prepare a proposal with an appropriate firm.

Angel Investors

Like a venture capitalist, this person will invest in your company possibly for stock or a share in the company, certainly for profits. Angel investors can appear in any form—venture capitalists, friends, partners, family—and are generally swayed by the same professional standards that a venture capitalist is. However, some may be swayed for other reasons, like friendship. Other angels will likely invest in growth potential small companies that are overlooked by the much more stringent and expectant venture capitalists and venture capital firms. Hence the name "angels." One source of angel capital is the SBA's ACE-NET program listed later in this chapter.

You may be able to get these people to invest in your company on the later agreement that they will receive stock. For example, if you offer $1000 investments, you can later promise to give 1000 shares of stock when you go public, or a certain percentage stake in the company. If you go this route, talk to a tax accountant for the federal tax consequences and an attorney for the legal requirements of your state.

Friends and Family

Often a small business can raise money through friends and family, especially at start-up. Again, you should treat these people with professionalism by explaining the potential risks and returns. When family and friends invest, they can be original stockholders or limited partners. Also, when you need more money or when you issue a direct public offering, they will be the first people you contact. If you run a SOHO business, this is an excellent source of start-up funds. Friends and family will be more likely to back you in one of these ventures than capitalists, the SBA, or bankers.

Bank Loans

The bank is often the first place small business starters think of when it comes to obtaining financing. While some banks offer loans to small businesses, some do not. It depends on the policy of the bank and the criteria they have established to loan money. Typically, a bank will loan money to a client if the client has collateral or has impeccable personal credit qualifications or can repay the loan with any ongoing income from other than the start-up business.

The criteria a bank will use to lend money is the amount and purpose of the loan; the primary and secondary sources of repaying the loan; the company data, such as management and operations; the financial data, including balance sheets and cash-flow statements; your personal credit history; and the reliability of the company. Any loan is usually secured by the equipment, personal or company assets, or land being purchased. However, that does not stop most banks from wanting you to be fully collateralized.

Getting a loan at a bank is difficult, we will tell you that up front. Most start-ups will not get them. However, if you can grow your business steadily over a period of time, banks will be more inclined to lend you money because you have proven you can operate your business. Many small business starters will simply have to grow first before approaching a bank. Smaller banks might be more apt to loan to a start-up or a SOHO business than a larger bank. Check local small banks for their policies.

Still, you may be able to get a loan. Some things to enhance your odds are to appear well-dressed and calm, to answer questions honestly and directly, and to have a great business plan. Circumlocution, stammering, and lying are not things you want to do in front of the loan officer. Remember, too, that honesty is the best policy. If the bank turns you down, you can try another bank. Some first-time business start-ups have gone to several if not dozens of banks before getting a loan. Have patience.

However, if you qualify for a loan, you will want to know a few types of loan products banks offer. These can vary by bank or by region. Loans are typically paid for in installment payments or in balloon payments, which are a combination of installment loans with a final large payment. Some banks offer seasonal credit and bridge loans to cover specific periods in the business year. Demand or promissory notes that are due at any time the bank demands might also be issued, but you will want to avoid one of those.

Here are some bank offerings:

1. **Revolving Lines of Credit**: Here you receive a line of credit payable over the course of, say, a year. Usually these are small amounts of between $5,000 and $50,000. You generally can use the credit as you need it and are charged only on what you use.

2. **Intermediate Term Debt**: These shorter-term loans are usually 60 months or less in duration, and they are

secured by collateral such as equipment purchased. These are good ways to get equipment.

3. **Term Loans**: These are used to generally acquire real estate and are typically amortized for up to 180 month periods. For small businesses, you will typically see loans up to the $100,000 mark.

A growing trend among larger banks such as Norwest is to offer businesses packages if they bank at that bank. These can include free checking, insurance, low minimum balances, ready lines of credit, ATM cards, and credit cards—all without a lot of paperwork and complicated statements. For a SOHO business, something like this is a great way to start.

Also, some cities have bank pools in which many banks pool resources to offer loans to more risky small businesses. Often your bank or your local economic development office can give you information on these.

Sell Some of Your Assets

Some people sell lake cottages, homes, cars, furniture, stamp/coin collections or other possessions to start their business. You will have to be careful here because you do not want to sell something you will want or need later on. The key here is to sell what you can, like a vacation home or a third car that no one in the family is using.

If you have stock options, or mutual funds at your current job, these can be sold to finance your new venture. It might not be prudent to dip into any IRAs for this purpose, though. Use your judgment. If you own another business, you might consider selling it in order to finance your new start-up. (See below for more on this).

Grants/Incentives

Sometimes foundations and government sources offer grants and incentives to small businesses. Local governments sometimes offer utility rate and property tax incentives for small businesses who employ locals. A city like Fort Wayne, Indiana has a Community Development Corporation that's in charge of helping small businesses through programs, loans, enterprise zones and assistance. See if your community has a similar agency. These agencies and programs can be a great source of information and capital.

Additionally, state and federal governments might offer tax benefits if you hire minorities, the disadvantaged, or teens during the summer. Check around. The Minority Business Development Agency was created to help minority business grow. It has nine regional centers. Anyone can benefit from locating in an Urban Enterprise Zone (UEZ). These are in disadvantaged parts of cities, and companies that set up shop there are offered tax incentives and government aid.

Also, minorities and women can benefit from grants issued by foundations and government. Some grants come from specific groups as awards for entrepreneurship. Others come from groups dedicated to helping those in similar circumstances. Black, Hispanic, Asian, and women's groups abound. Simply check your local phone book for a list of supporting groups. Sometimes your local government can give you further information. Chapter twelve has resources as well.

Small Business Administration

The Federal Government has a variety of departments and programs to aid small businesses, most notably through the Small Business Administration. Additionally, as we mentioned above, it has some programs to aid minorities and women-owned small businesses. In addition to loans, it offers assistance in business plan writing, financial accounting, management, manufacturing, retail, taxes, and other areas.

One unique and new source of SBA financial assistance is the Angel Capital Electronic Network—ACENET. This is an Internet-based program that allows cash-strapped high-growth potential businesses to "advertise" their companies to angel investors who sign up for the program. The angels invest in these companies, many too small for venture capital firms to touch. You can find more information and register your company for this program on the SBA Web site at *www.gov/advo/acenet.html*.

However, let's look at some of the SBA loans that might help you raise capital. The SBA operates a loan program for small business including several different types of loans. Since the purpose of the SBA is to promote small businesses, it uses the loan program for that end. The SBA has a portfolio of $27 billion in loans to over 180,000 small businesses. It has guaranteed loans in which the SBA guarantees 75-90% of the loan you get from a bank and direct loans in which the SBA offers market-rate loans for those unable to secure bank capital.

- SBA's 7(a) Loan Guarantee Program, which finances small businesses through a variety of specialize loan programs including LowDoc, FA$TRAK, CAPLines, International Trade, Export Working Capital, Pollution Control, DELTA, Minority and Women's Prequal, Disabled Assistance, Qualified Employee Trusts and Veteran's Loans. All of these can be further examined at the SBA Web site: *www.sba.gov*. Or write the SBA for information or go to a local SBA office.
- SBA's Microloan Program finances businesses through intermediaries, usually providing loans from $100 to $25,000. An ideal source for micro businesses or SOHO businesses without extravagant capital requirements.
- SBA's Certified Development Company (504 Loan) Program makes long-term loans for equipment and land, and for interest on an interim loan. Terms are up to twenty years with low downpayments. These are often administered by local government.
- SBA's Small Business Investment Company Program is an amalgam of companies licensed and regulated by SBA and provides venture capital to start-up a small business. These are located throughout the country.
- One Stop Capital Shops gather local, state, and federal agencies in one location to address the financial needs of small businesses. There are locations in about thirteen states. Check your state for a location.
- The Certified and Preferred Lenders, Secondary Market, and Surety Bond programs round out the list.

Be sure to write the SBA for complete information. A call or visit to an SBA office, Small Business Development Center or SCORE office will expedite your search. The SBA also has loan application forms on its Web site for downloading.

Partners

Taking in additional partners either in the form of fellow incorporators or limited partners is another method of raising capital. Often an investor will agree to become a limited partner on the strength of your plan and you personally. In this situation, your partner is strictly a financial backer. He or she will want to see a return on investment but will not want to participate in any of the work of the company. This can be an ideal situation if you do not want to sell stock or incorporate and if you have some backers already. Finding limited partners could be difficult, though, if you have to search for them. The laws of your state may not permit advertising for them, so you will have to network in order to find them. Often these will be friends, family members, business associates, college friends, or others who have a professional or personal connection to you or any other principals in your company.

Business Networking/Brand Name Sharing

This is where one or more businesses combine to share one brand name, although each produces different goods. For example, let's say a group of automotive suppliers cannot get their products on shelves. They sign an agreement, put the common brand and logo on all products, and use a combined marketing/distribution system to place the goods. This really works and can increase each participant company's market share dramatically.

Although this is not capital per se, it is a way to get more out of your capital dollars and a way to raise your market share/product awareness. It is also a way to increase cash flow and revenues, which is one of the prime ways to attract traditional bank and SBA loans.

Barter

Business barter exchanges are relatively new and growing. Here you will exchange your good or service for other goods and services with participating companies. You might sell your product for free accounting from an accountant or for auto work on your company vehicle from a garage. Many local exchanges have been set up. If your city has one, simply call them or drop by for some information.

The tax implications of a barter exchange is something to consider, as is the fact that you are not getting capital in the traditional sense. It is more like working capital in the form of goods/services received—virtual capital. Still, this can get you services and products that otherwise you would have to part with capital to receive. It might cut into your profitability but it will enable you to run your business with less start-up money.

Use Another Business's Assets

Maybe you have one part-time business with cash flow but limited growth opportunities. This business could provide eventual start-up capital for a future business with much more growth potential.

Part-Time/Seasonal Job

A part-time job before, during or after your start-up can provide capital and will be proof to potential investors and lenders that you are serious about financing your business. Although you will not raise a lot of money this way, it is a viable option, especially if you are starting a SOHO or micro business.

You may be privy to other sources of capital such as inheritance, stock, garage sale revenue, or rainy-day money stuffed into a mason jar. We are getting pretty far-fetched here for a reason. We want you to search for capital in any and every avenue or venue possible. Do not overlook any potential legal source of capital.

If you receive a bank loan or capital from other people, you must keep the bank or investors informed of your company's progress. A banker should see monthly financials, including your cash flow statements, balance sheets, and receivables. Also, explain the things the loan is doing for your company in terms of inventory, marketing, personnel, capital purchases, and/or sales. The financials are more important, though. Your banker is, in essence, a partner who has a vested interest in your company. It is worth your while to work *with* him or her before, during, and after getting a loan.

Send your stock investors annual reports from you at the end of the fiscal year. We suggest you provide quarterly or monthly updates as well, explaining what the company did the past month or months. Investors will appreciate these updates. Additionally, you are required to hold stockholder's meetings which you should do on an annual basis. You will invite your investors to the meeting and discuss the company's progress thus far, vote on issues, and get a chance to talk face-to-face to your backers. Hold it on a Saturday so everyone can come.

If you are unable to raise any capital, you might have to revise your business plan or put your venture on hold. Again, the best way of getting money is to first make some. That's why most businesses must start small. Do not give up, though. Some companies have started small and grown huge, and some have started big and failed. In essence, capital is very important, but must be used properly in conjunction with your plan and your goals.

Chapter 9

Unpleasant Business

Taxes and Insurance

We started the last chapter with two cliches. We will start this one with just one. Two things are certain in life—death and taxes. The latter is something you must come to grips with right away, and the former is dealt with through insurance. All fits in nicely, doesn't it. Well, it is not that simple, but you get the point.

Both of these can heap burdensome costs upon your small business, but they are usually unavoidable. In fact, taxes are unavoidable. Insurance is trickier. You may or may not need certain types for your business and employees. This is where the accountant and especially the insurance agent come in handy to explain the particulars of taxes and insurance and the associated costs of each. Let's examine the issues of taxes and insurance.

Taxes

The particulars of tax effects on small businesses is probably not lost on you. We mentioned earlier that taxes can affect your start-up entity election and are a great source of consternation to small business owners. Every one of you has paid taxes before, but probably not like you will pay them while you run your small business. And paying them yourself makes you understand more fully the consequences of taxes on your bottom line.

In fact, most business owners cite regulations and taxes as being among the biggest hindrances to business. This is because both sap money and resources from your company. Although we could argue the fairness of taxing very small businesses at all (we feel there should be a minimum floor to reach before your small business is taxed), the fact is taxes are with us and we have to work with them. If you are diligent, you can make some of the tax laws and the deductions work for you. You will therefore want to include your plan for dealing with taxes in your business plan and include them as costs of business.

Several things can affect your small business tax requirements. Your business entity type election will have the greatest effect. A corporation is taxed twice, while sole proprietors, partnerships, limited liability companies, and S-corporations are taxed only once on earnings. A small business with employees will incur greater withholding, and the employer will be forced to pay a share of the employee's social security tax. Also, certain regulated businesses have fees and extra taxation to contend with, including special business licenses. State and local taxes and fees might include utility fees, property taxes, county and city taxes, and sales taxes. Here, the amount affecting your small business depends on whether you have property or an office/plant. Another consideration is the state you live in. All sales, property, and income taxes vary from state to state and from city to city. Additionally, some businesses incur greater tax and fee burdens than others. Larger firms incur more burdens than simple SOHO businesses.

An accountant will be able to tell you in advance of the many tax consequences of each business election, so be sure to consult one. Taxes affect your start-up, because they will eat into your capital and will be a fixed cost. We feel that an accountant should also do your year-end taxes in order to provide you with the most deduction relief. Also, an accountant might be able to help you obtain tax relief through federal minority programs, certain employment programs, local economic development initiatives, and urban enterprise zones.

There are several basic types of taxes your business might incur. Federal taxes include Social Security taxes, Federal Unemployment taxes, income withholding, and business income taxes. State taxes include income withholding, sales/use taxes, and business income taxes. Local taxes usually include your property tax and sometimes a county economic development tax or a city income tax. The following is a more in-depth discussion of each form of taxation.

Social Security Taxes (FICA)

Anyone employing people is responsible for Social Security taxes. You even owe for yourself (called the Self-Employment Tax). The current tax rate is 7.65% for employees and the employer pays 7.65 percent. As your own employee, you will pay a 15.3% self-employed tax. Payment is due each quarter, unless you have over $5000 of tax. An accountant will help you with that.

The tax has two parts: old age, survivors, and disability insurance—OASDI; and Hospital Insurance—HI, often just called Medicare. OASDI is 6.2% for the first $65,400 in wages and HI is 1.45% on *all* income. Most small businesses will pay quarterly returns, but some may have to pay monthly. A few small ones where the owner works on it part-time and does not take a paycheck may be responsible for only a yearly return on income at that time.

Federal Unemployment Taxes (FUTA)

This tax is a quarterly tax for compensation to workers who have lost jobs through a variety of reasons. It is collected and then used in unemployment payments after an employee has been laid off. Its current rate is 6.2% and applies to the first $7,000 in wages you pay per year. After that you have no further burden.

Additionally, your state may require you to file a report with it listing your tax liability. Contact your state for information on unemployment tax.

Income Withholding Taxes

Withholding is something we are all familiar with. If you employee people or pay yourself, you will be responsible for using government formulas to determine income withholding amounts on each paycheck. Partners, sole proprietors, limited liability company members, or shareholders may be required to pay quarterly estimated taxes to the government on a Form 1040-ES. Other businesses such as corporations with many employees will pay quarterly withholding taxes on federal Form 941.

The current tax law has the following personal tax rates: 15%, 28%, 31%, and 36%. A 10% surtax on higher incomes pushes the top marginal rate to a little over 39%

State and local income withholding taxes vary. New Hampshire pays nothing, while the rate in North Dakota is 12%. Your state will fall somewhere in between. You will generally pay the same way as you do for federal taxes—quarterly with a "coupon" that you send to the state revenue department. Check your state revenue office for further information.

Business Income Taxes

Corporations are the only entity taxed twice, once at the corporate level and once at the stockholder's level. All other forms enjoy single taxation at the stockholder, partner or owner level, usually paying a capital gains tax or a simple personal income tax. Much of this income is taxed as ordinary income and is done generally on either Form 1040 Schedule C or 1040 Schedule D. For instance, sole proprietors report income on their 1040 Form and on Schedule C or C-EZ. Partnerships report it on their 1040 and on Form 1065. Limited liability companies will report their business income on their regular income tax form and on Form 1065. Corporations will report income on Form 1120 or 1120A. S-corporations file it on Form 1120S. Federal corporate tax rates range from 15% to 35%. The appendix has a complete list of corporate state tax rates.

Most states have income taxes for corporations and some might for other entities such as partnerships and limited liability companies. These laws change constantly so the best bet here is to contact your state for its requirements. You might want to call your state's Small Business Development Center for information as well.

Sales and Use Tax

These are taxes on the sale of goods or services. Most will be state taxes, although some cities have sales taxes. You will need to collect sales tax depending on your state requirements (some states have no sales tax). Use taxes on out-of-state purchases used in your state are a further burden. Most states will require you to pay these use taxes in a similar manner to your sales taxes. Some states will also levy excise taxes on such things as sales of gasoline, liquor, and tobacco.

Sales taxes can be exempt on purchases you make with the intent of reselling the goods. The tax will be due when you sell the goods to the consumer. If you resell what you purchase you will receive a sales tax exemption. This number is filed for when you register your business with your revenue department. Most forms have check-off boxes allowing you to apply for a variety of taxes and for *exemption*. After you get the exemption, most states will have you fill out exempt forms every time you purchase goods this way. You give this form to the seller and pay no sales tax until you resell the goods.

Most small businesses will pay monthly or quarterly estimated or actual sales tax, depending on sales volume and amount owed. The state will likely give you a "coupon" booklet or sheet with statements you fill out and submit with your check. More and more states are moving to electronic fund transfer to accomplish this.

Excise taxes are other forms of state taxes and will affect certain businesses, including wholesalers and retailers. Your state or SBDC can provide more information.

Property Taxes

If you own your office or factory, you will naturally owe property taxes on your land and your plant/office. These vary from state to state. Most are paid to your county or township assessor's office either yearly or twice a year. Some are paid through mortgages.

Inventory Taxes

One particularly heinous tax is the inventory tax. This is a tax due on your inventory of goods in say a warehouse or factory at a specific time of the year. You inventory your goods and then submit a form and a check to the state. The idea is to tax the goods you have not sold yet. Brilliant, huh? Some states are doing away with these taxes, and we hope all will eventually.

The only good news for businesses is that some states have done away with inventory taxes, some sales taxes, and many have lowered vehicle excise taxes and property taxes due to other sources of revenue, notably gaming and lottery proceeds. Still, the effect of taxes is still great.

To pay taxes, use the coupon booklets the federal government or your state sends you. If you are not sent one, you are still responsible to pay taxes. Talk to your accountant about this. Some states send envelopes, forms, and explanations on state withholding when a business is formed. The federal government will send forms for quarterly taxes.

Most companies, except sole proprietors, will file for a Federal Employer Identification Number (IRS FORM SS-4) that registers you with the IRS. Take your Federal ID number with you to register for state sales, excise, and withholding taxes. If you do not have it when you register, you may be able to send it to the state revenue office later. Check your state's requirements to see if the FEIN is even needed for state registration if you are a sole proprietor.

If you sell a good, you must record sales tax for the state in which the good is sold. If you sell via mail, collect only tax from residents of the state in which your business exists. Again, to purchase merchandise for resale, you will need a state sales tax exemption number. In some states, your sales tax number allows you to buy merchandise without paying sales tax. Once you re-sell it, the tax is collected by you. In some states, when you collect sales tax, you keep a percentage because you are acting as the *collection agent* for that tax. This is not true in all cases, but in many. Consult your state for its requirements.

Remember, most taxes (social security, withholding) must be deposited quarterly if the total is $500 or more. The IRS will send you a coupon booklet—Form 8109—for your quarterly tax returns. In addition, Form 941 will also be sent for quarterly returns. Form 940 EZ or 940 will be sent for year-end FUTA tax returns, due January 31. W2s are due to the employee at the end of January, and the federal copy is due at the IRS on February 28. The states generally send simple forms and envelopes for withholding taxes and sales tax, although recently some have switched to an electronic transfer system for withholding over a certain amount. This money is automatically transferred from your bank to the state. Check with your state.

Business tax returns, such as for income, are due within four months after the company's tax year ends. This is important to remember. So, if you do not get them by mid-January, write for them, or better, go to your accountant. The following are some of the tax guides published by the IRS. We suggest you write the IRS to obtain all of them. Publication 15 (Circular E)—Employer's Tax Guide—is an excellent publication and is usually sent to the company. However, we suggest that you write the IRS for a copy while doing your research. In addition, write for the Small Business Tax Kit—SBTK— which contains several publications.

   1 Your Rights as a Taxpayer
  15 Circular E, Employer's Tax Guide
 334 Tax Guide for Small Business
 463 Travel, Entertainment, Gift and Car Expenses
 501 Exemptions, Standard Deduction, and Filing Information
 502 Medical and Dental Expenses
 505 Tax Withholding and Estimated Tax
 509 Tax Calendars
 510 Excise Taxes
 529 Miscellaneous Deductions
 533 Self-Employment Tax
 534 Depreciation
 535 Business Expenses
 536 Net Operating Losses
 537 Installment Sales
 538 Accounting Periods and Methods
 541 Tax Information on Partnerships
 542 Tax Information on Corporations
 544 Sales and Other Dispositions of Assets
 550 Investment Income and Expenses
 552 Recordkeeping for Individuals
 560 Retirement Plans for the Self-Employed
 575 Pension and Annuity Income
 583 Taxpayers Starting a Business
 587 Business Use of Your Home
 589 Tax Information on S-corporations

590 Individual Retirement Arrangements (IRAs)
594 The Collection Process (Employment Tax Accounts)
724 Help Other People with Their Tax Returns
901 U.S. Tax Treaties
908 Bankruptcy and Other Debt Cancellation
910 Guide to Free Tax Services
      (Has a list of all publications)
911 Tax Information for Direct Sellers
937 Employment Taxes and Information Returns
1004 Identification Numbers Under ERISA
1057 Small Business Tax Education Program
1244 Employee's Daily Record of Tips
1544 Reporting Cash Payments of Over $10,000

Understanding taxes is one of the cornerstones of business success. Being unfamiliar with new tax laws, the numerous deductions, allowances, etc., can cost you thousands of dollars over the years and many lost work hours. In order to take advantage of these great money saving deductions and allowances, we suggest a competent tax accountant, studying deductions/allowances, reading books, and utilizing the existing IRS services.

An accountant will help you take advantage of the following full or partial tax deductions:

- Lawyer's fees against liability claims
- Accounting expenses for audits, bookkeeping, and tax return preparation
- Business taxes, except federal income taxes, are deductible
- Cars used in the business (or your car if it is used for business)
- Bank account charges (for checking account)
- Charitable contributions
- Depreciation
- Repairs
- Insurance premiums
- Interest on business loans
- Business loses and bad debts
- Office rent

- Maintenance
- Salaries
- Merchandise costs
- Travel expenses when conducted for business
- Uniforms
- Social Security taxes paid by you for employees
- Office expenses and supplies
- Salaries
- Dues to business organizations
- Small business owner health insurance premiums

Proper tax planning includes setting up the right business entity, using deductions, setting realistic goals, maintaining cash flow, and keeping expenses low. By making it a habit to read newspaper, magazine, and journal articles on taxes, you and your company stand a better chance of being abreast of tax changes. Changes in tax laws occur annually.

Numerous books and software programs exist for tax preparation and information. Chapter twelve lists some.

The SBA and IRS offer ways in which the entrepreneur can brush up on their tax knowledge. The SBA often holds seminars, and the IRS has the Volunteer Income Tax Assistance. This program gives you the opportunity to keep current on tax regulations while helping others with their tax returns. IRS instructors teach you how to prepare such forms as the 1040EZ, 1040A, and the basic 1040 at no cost to you except your time. This is a great educational program.

Another IRS program is called the Small Business Tax Education Program. This program is specifically designed for the self-employed and the small business owner. According to IRS publication 1057, instructors will teach you such vital information as:

- What records to keep and for how long
- How to use Federal Tax Deposit Coupons and how to fill out other business and employment tax forms
- Technical information on a series of selected tax topics pertinent to a small business
- What other help is available and how to get it
- The role of the IRS and how to deal effectively with the various offices of the IRS

Finally, most states hold tax seminars for new and growing businesses. These are often run by the SBA or the Small Business Development Centers. Write your state revenue office for more information.

Insurance

Insurance is another matter to take seriously. For the new small office, home office company, the needs may be minimal. You may need insurance just for yourself or for inventory. However, larger small businesses may need a wide range of insurance covering inventory, liability, theft, employee health and life plans, workers' compensation insurance. Many companies with full-time employees provide some semblance of health insurance and sick time benefits. Often this is a combination of employee and employer contributions on the insurance side.

The best thing to do in regard to insurance is talk with both your accountant and an insurance agent (or several to "shop around"). Together, the three of you must determine what your needs will be, since needs vary between entities. Needs also vary in specific businesses. For example, two stores of similar nature may need different insurance. Both will need insurance against theft, fire, or other damage to inventory or property. But one store may offer health insurance and the other not.

One main consideration for the start-up business is maintaining life and health insurance for yourself. If you have another job, you might be covered. Or you could go onto your spouses plan. When you plan for your business, you will have to come to terms with what insurance you personally need and what is needed by your business. We mentioned already that insurance needs vary by business, and that's true. The requirements of a SOHO business might be minimal compared to those of a manufacturing concern. However, a SOHO business involved in a profession like accounting might need liability insurance. And a small retail shop will need inventory and possibly business property insurance. With employees comes the added responsibilities of health and life insurance, unemployment taxes, and liability insurance.

The key with insurance is to be covered no matter what. No one likes making insurance payments, but there comes a time when some among us will say "I'm glad I did." We hope that's not you. Insurance needs are as varied as businesses, so *consult a professional such as an accountant or insurance agent when you start your business.* Do not get caught unaware.

Chapter 10

The Ties That Bind

Regulations and Licenses

The previous chapter outlined the burden of taxes on the small business. Regulations—and to a smaller extent licensing requirements—are also part and parcel of the external government influences and restrictions on small business. They have influence over how we employ, produce, and sell goods and how we develop our companies. Most regulations were enacted to redress a real or perceived wrong, threat, or inequality. Over the years, a steady stream of government regulations have been enacted so that now literally hundreds if not thousands of local, state, and federal regulations face business owners.

Despite the overwhelming amount of regulations, they have in essence become a part of doing business like paying taxes and giving out sales receipts. They must be dealt with as a hindrance but not a blockage to doing business. If your company grows, sooner or later most simple regulations will cease to have a negative effect on the company. But that's when other regulations start affecting your business and especially your employment and benefits practices. No one business can get around all regulations, but not all regulations apply to any one business. The key is to not panic but to deal with regulations in constructive ways.

Most small business owners would agree that government regulations are often the main cause of headaches for new businesspersons. There are local, state, and federal regulations that affect everything from employment to taxes to pollution to products to advertising to worker safety to prices to warranties to communications. Most industries have industry-specific regulations to adhere to, many environmental in nature. Other regulations like minimum wages affect almost all employers, large and small. Your lawyer should inform you of those pertaining to your business. Local and state regulations are somewhat easier to deal with because your chance at redress are greater with local sources of regulations. Laws made in Washington are hard to argue about or discuss, but it is much easier to talk to local or state lawmakers and regulators.

Still, many small business owners will face a simple set of regulations that are definitely surmountable. These include local zoning laws, start-up bureaucracy and simple wage rules. Plan on dealing with these and other regulations before you start your business. Detail your strategies in either your business plan or in a separate, personal notebook. That way you can face them as they arise.

City and county zoning laws were created to keep residential, commercial, and industrial sites in specific areas of communities. When you start your business, you must adhere to these laws, especially if you have a home office. As long as you are not having clients over or are not creating too much business activity from your home office, you should be fine. If you need to use the office for more than paperwork, you can ask for a zoning variance from your local government.

Start-up bureaucracy, includes the forms, rules, and fees you must pay to simply start business. The requirements vary depending on business entity type. Corporations are relatively complex and expensive to start compared to sole proprietors. Most of the regulations in starting a business have to do with liability protection, company officer registration, and capital (stocks). The only real regulations here are registering everything in proper format with the proper fees.

Most small businesses will adhere to minimum wage laws and mandated Social Security benefits withholding. These are not so much a hindrance as a cost. Still, the minimum is only $5.15/hour, which should not break anyone's bank. Simply plan for the inclusion of each in your wage and benefit plan. Since size plays a big part in determining the amount of regulations affecting a business. Many regulations like the Family and Medical Leave Act are valid only for businesses employing a certain number of people. Many small businesses will be unaffected by these acts. However, you should keep these and other regulations in mind as you plan future growth and then as you grow. You may choose to adhere to certain non-binding regulations because of size, it might make good business sense to do so out of principle or for ethical reasons. This puts you in a good light with employees, the community, and customers.

Along with regulations come licensing requirements. If you incorporate in any of the regulated professions, seek legal, governmental, and published sources of information *before* you incorporate. These professions include accountants, bankers, insurance, doctors and dentists, engineering, hotels, lawyers, real estate agents, liquor stores, teachers, detectives, and restaurants just to name a tiny fraction. Be sure to check with your state department of commerce on your chosen field. Many require licenses or special testing in order to do business as a licensed professional. Professional engineers must pass a rigorous test in order to be called "Professional Engineers." Accountants must pass the Certified Public Accountant test, which is also rigorous. Bars and often restaurants must obtain liquor licenses. Builders and contractors must often be bonded. Private investigators are licensed. Doctors are certified by state boards.

Licensing occurs at the state level and is usually handled by a state agency(ies). Sometimes licenses are required at the city level, so check with the city clerk.

These local, state, and federal regulations must all be taken into account whenever you plan a business. The more you understand and work with the regulations, the better your chances for success. As a business, there are several laws and acts to protect consumers. The Federal Trade Commission Act (unfair trade), Fair Packaging and Labeling Act, Mansion-Moss Warranty Act (a grand-daddy law that concerns warranties), UCC-the Uniform Commercial Code (sales contracts), the Truth in Lending Act (disclosure of credit terms), and the Fair Credit Reporting Act (protection of personal credit).

In addition, as a prospective employer, you must be aware of the numerous laws that federal and state governments have passed regarding labor, safety, and a variety of other issues. There are taboos in many areas of employment such as discrimination and asking illegal questions in interviews. Knowing employment laws is as important as knowing tax laws. You do not want to get burned by accidentally breaking the law in your first time as a business owner.

Some regulations are non-enforceable and voluntary. These include joining the Better Business Bureau, the Chamber of Commerce, trade groups, or associations. Many of these have ethical tomes and requirements that businesses must follow in order to be a member in good standing.

We have listed some important regulations and laws you should know. Again, consult an attorney or the Chamber of Commerce or your county law library for more in-depth treatment of regulatory laws, or call the agencies we list below. Some of these laws will not apply to all businesses, however they are all good ethical guides to follow. In fact, you might be able to include some of the concepts and ideas of regulations in your company or employee handbook. An employee handbook will be able to enumerate and detail the company's rules, ethics, and procedures. If you plan to hire employees, work on a handbook while writing your business plan.

Most employers will have to follow the FLSA act, the OSHA rules, the ERISA act provisions, and other regulations. All should follow fair employment practices.

Fair Wages

- **Fair Labor Standards Act (FLSA)**—Sets the minimum wage at $5.15 an hour, provides for overtime pay past forty hours per week and sets restrictions on child labor.
- **Contract Work Hours Safety Standards Act of 1962**—Provides for time and a half paid for work over forty hours per weak.
- **Equal Pay Act of 1963**—Prohibits discrimination in pay base on sex.
- **Walsh-Healy Act**—Sets minimum wages for federal contractors of $10,000 or over.
- **Davis-Bacon Act**—Minimum wage for federally-funded projects of $2,000.

Equal Opportunity/Civil Rights

- **Civil Rights Act of 1964**—This makes it unlawful for employers with fifteen or more employees to discriminate against people based on race, color, religion, national origin, or sex in regards to hiring and employment.
- **Age Discrimination in Employment Act of 1967**—Prohibits firms with 20 or more employees from discriminating against workers 40 or over.
- **Equal Employment Opportunity Act of 1972**—Prohibits firms with twenty or more employees from discriminating against them on race, color, sex, national origin, or religion.
- **Pregnancy Discrimination Act of 1978**—Requires same treatment of pregnancy as other medical reasons.
- **Vocational Rehabilitation Act of 1973**—Prohibits discrimination against physically or mentally handicapped persons in federal contracts.
- **Vietnam Era Veterans' Readjustment Act of 1974**—Prohibits federal contractors with $10,000 of work from discriminating against Vietnam veterans.
- **Immigration and Reform Act of 1986**—Employers must verify proof of citizenship and legal residency in the United States of employees. Each employer must keep a completed federal I-9 form for each employee hired after 1986. This is an important business requirement.
- **Americans with Disabilities Act of 1990**—Prohibits employers with fifteen or more employees from discriminating against handicapped persons and to provide them accommodations that do not pose an undue hardship.
- **Older Workers Benefit Protection Act of 1990**—Prohibits discrimination with respect to employee benefits based on age, and regulates early retirement benefits.

Worker Safety

- **Occupational Safety And Health Act of 1970 (OSHA)**—Employers must provide safe working conditions for workers. An addition to OSHA is the Hazard Communication Standard, which is a system of informing employees on hazards and how to respond to them.

Labor Relations

- **National Labor Relations Act of 1935 (The Wagner Act)**—Gives employees the right to unionize.
- **Taft-Hartley Act of 1947**—Balances rights of employers and unions in relation to rights and negotiations.
- **Landrum-Griffin Act of 1957**—Gives rights to union members within the union.

Fair Treatment

- **Employee Polygraph Protection Act of 1988**—Makes it unlawful for employers to request polygraph lie detector tests from employees or job applicants.
- **Worker Adjustment and Retraining Notification Act of 1988 (WARN)**—States that employers must give sixty days warning if they plan to close the plant or lay off workers.
- **Worker Compensation Laws**—These books from state to state. The requirements and benefits vary. Check your state for its worker compensation law.
- **Whistleblower Protection Statutes of 1989**—Protects employees of financial institutions and government contractors from retaliating against employees who report violations of the law.

Benefits

- **Family and Medical Leave Act of 1991**—Provides employees of companies with fifty or more employees up to twelve weeks of unpaid, and in some cases paid, leave to care for sick children, relatives, or themselves.
- **Employee Retirement Income Security Act of 1974**—Governs operation of pension and retirement benefits provided by private employers.

Some regulations must be clearly posted in many places of employment. The minimum wage and the fair employment posters must generally be posted. In some states, others are mandatory. For example, North Dakota mandates the following be posted for employees: Federal and North Dakota Minimum Wage posters, Workers Compensation Safety and Fraud Hotline poster, Job Service North Dakota poster, Employee Polygraph Protection Act poster, Job Safety and Health Protection poster, Equal Employment Opportunity is THE LAW poster, and Family Medical Leave Act posters.

Your state will have its own list. Again, many of these posters can be obtained at one of these numerous government regulatory bodies or through your state department of labor. Check around.

Regulatory Agencies and Phone Numbers

- Department of Agriculture—(202) 690-1516
- Department of Commerce—(202) 482-4144
- Department of Labor—(202) 219-9148
- Environmental Protection Agency—(202) 260-5480
- Internal Revenue Service—(202) 622-4989
- Securities and Exchange Commission—(202) 942-2950
- SBA Office of National Ombudsman (312) 353-0880

The SBA's Web site has some more information on regulations. Visit it at *www.sba.gov/regfair.*

As you can see, regulations can be sticky indeed. Try to keep current with them, and you will not get hurt by them. Whatever you do, do not intentionally break the law just to make a few more dollars. It is not worth the fines, embarrassment, or even loss of your company. Make the regulations work for you, and you will have eliminated one of the biggest headaches to businesspersons.

Worksheet: Regulations

Use this worksheet to list regulations you, your attorney, accountant, or advisor have determined relate to your business. Also list any special licenses you may need.

Regulations

1. _____
2. _____
3. _____
4. _____
5. _____
6. _____
7. _____
8. _____
9. _____
10. _____
11. _____
12. _____

Licenses Needed

1. _____
2. _____
3. _____
4. _____
5. _____

Planning for Tomorrow
A Brief Guide to Small Business Strategic Planning

Thus far we have concentrated on starting a business. While many issues such as taxation, regulations, and business plans deal with start-up and beyond, most of our efforts have dealt with start-up. Although that's the purpose and aim of our book, we feel that the issue of strategic planning is so important to your post start-up operations that we included this chapter. After your business is running, you will need to modify your initial business plan to meet your current needs. These needs could be growth, contraction, financial, or otherwise. Thus, a consideration at start-up is the effect of changes affecting your business and the economy. This chapter is designed to introduce you to the concept of strategic planning and to present the many ways planning can help business growth and profitability.

More worldwide competition and cheaper labor markets, and more business start-ups all affect business. These pressures need to be addressed if your business is to survive. By regularly addressing them, you will learn to apply creative solutions to current and upcoming problems. That's the real beauty of strategic planning: it allows you to plan the future. The point here is that you do not want to be eighty years old and still mumbling about what *could* or *should* have been. Strategic planning will enable you to do what *needs* to be done.

Strategic planning is simply the ongoing process of planning for your small business. In one way or another, every business must undergo strategic planning, regardless of size. Its importance becomes clear once the outside pressures on your business begin to become apparent and the lessons of running a business are learned. Your initial business plan was meant to get your business started and to act as a template for future—two, three, five year—growth. That initial template may be fine in a general or macro sense, but on the specific or micro level, it needs tweaking. That's where the concept of planning comes into play. Planning will tell you what is right and what is wrong with your small business.

You will learn to recognize those parts of your plan (and goals) that are not working or were unrealistic in the first place. In other words, those areas where you need more effort, improvements, or attention. These areas have either failed to produce the desired results, or they simply need updating to meet the current state of your business, the economy, or your goals. The key here is to minimize your weaknesses.

Planning will also benefit your understanding of what you are doing right, what areas of your small business have been successful. An important part of the ongoing strategic planning is recognizing your strengths and enhancing them. After all, any strength or expertise that becomes apparent is beneficial to your company. You will want to concentrate on exploiting these strengths.

A strategic plan enables you to review your short and long-term goals. These are the milestones you are determined to reach as a business owner. Sometimes they must be revised, changed, or eliminated. By planning, you can determine what goals need refinement or elimination. Planning allows you the choice to determine how you will reach these goals based on your current and future business status. It also forces you to examine why those goals were unreachable or why you achieved them.

As we mentioned earlier, all businesses should conduct strategic planning at least once a year. SOHO businesses can use strategic planning sessions in order to facilitate growth, evaluate the benefits of the home office, and to identify changes or obstacles in the environment. For instance, having a home office is stressful because of the family life also occurring there. Thus you might revise your plan to move up to an office.

Or not. That's right. You may recognize a problem and still decide to do nothing about it. In planning, you get that choice. Not every problem needs to be addressed, because problems are relative, and their importance to your operations may not warrant any actions. When you complete your planning sessions you will be able to tell where your efforts should be expended.

The keys to strategic planning are recognition, formulation, implementation, and evaluation. The first step is recognizing what happened to your company in the past six months to a year. The second is formulating strategies to enhance your progress and address your problems. Next, you will implement strategies and objectives meant to achieve new and existing goals. Finally, you evaluate—next year—the results of your new strategies.

Sometimes you have to review your progress monthly or quarterly. That's fine. You can fine tune or adjust your business plan at those times. Also, you can get an earlier glimpse of the success or failure of your strategies. Again, you will be the one to determine when and how you review your strategy implementation.

The following outline examines a typical strategic plan. It is used to determine your strengths and weaknesses, opportunities and threats, and to formulate actions meant to enhance or nullify them respectively. After you have gone through your initial planning session, you can then use the new strategic plan to rewrite or revise your current business plan. This is useful, especially if you plan growth and need financing. The strategic plan can aid and enhance the business plan, making the chances of security financing all the better.

At the end of every year, perform a strategic evaluation of your company. If your company is small, probably the whole staff will be involved. If you have grown, the board of directors and top management will want to perform this duty jointly.

We suggest the following plan. For each section, complete the information as best you can using all resources available to you. This will take some time, so do not try and rush through.

Strategic Planning Outline

I. Introduction
   - Introduction
   - Issues Pertaining to Your Company
   - Mission Statement
   - Current Objectives

III. Strengths of Your Company
   - Management and Operations
   - Marketing
   - Finance and Accounting

III. Weaknesses of Your Company
   - Management and Operations
   - Marketing
   - Finance and Accounting

IV. Analysis
   - Competitor Analysis
   - Key Ingredients Matrix
   - Opportunities for Your Company
   - Threats to Your Company

V. New Strategic Plan
   - Redefined Mission Statement
   - New Company Objectives
   - Possible Strategies
   - Chosen Strategies
   - Implementation of Chosen Strategies
   - Strategic Evaluation

VI. Appendixes, Bibliography, Indexes

Now let's examine each section of this sample strategic plan. At the end of this chapter is a list of SBA publications that might be of further assistance. One thing to remember is to use this strategic plan to review the work you have done this year and to plan for next year. A plan can help you determine your needs in all areas, including financial. You might decide to pursue a loan after this plan, or to make a stock offering. Maybe you will decide to grow or expand into different areas. Whatever you decide, remember that your plan will guide you for the next year or so.

Introduction

This is the front material for your plan. You will want to complete the four parts with care, however. They will be used to determine new objectives and mission statements.

- **Introduction**—Briefly describe your company. Since the strategic plan is for you, do not include a lot of detail, but cover those things that have changed since your first business plan.
- **Issues Pertaining to Your Company**—List those economic, political, and social issues at the moment that affect your company directly.
- **Mission Statement**—Write your original Mission Statement here. Later, you might change it.
- **Current Objectives**—What are your objectives or goals, now? In other words, list your objectives when you wrote your first business plan.

Strengths of Your Company

Here you will make lists of the positive things that happened to you this year. Your strengths will be self-evident, but listing them will help later when you determine new goals and strategies.

- **Management and Operations**—Where, what, and who are your strengths in your company's management? List the things you did right this year. Be honest here and do not try to build your management style or your operations up.
- **Marketing**—Where and what are your marketing strengths? What worked this year, what were the reasons you sold good? What advertising and distribution systems do you credit?
- **Finance and Accounting**—Where and what are your finance/accounting strengths? How did you use your capital to generate business?

Weaknesses of Your Company

This section is similar to the one above, except it lists your weaknesses. These are areas where you recognize the need for improvement or that were deficient in your past year. Weaknesses are important to note, because they are the areas you will want to strengthen and improve next year.

- **Management and Operations**—Where, what, and who are your weaknesses in running the company? Why are these weaknesses? Are you able to keep up with demand?
- **Marketing**—Where and what are your marketing weaknesses? What marketing/advertising did not work? How did your distribution channels suit your business?
- **Finance and Accounting**—Where and what are your finance/accounting weaknesses? If you needed more capital, note it here. Do your credit policies work? Is there a constant cash flow?

Analysis

This section analyzes competitors and yourself. You need to be thorough here, because you will use these ingredients along with the previous analysis to determine your new strategies.

- **Competitor Analysis**—Who are your competitors, and how are they doing? Did they succeed last year? Did they cost you business?
- **Key Ingredients Matrix**—What are the key ingredients for success in your business? List as many factors you can think of. You will soon use these key ingredients in conjunction with your upcoming SWOT (Strength/Weaknesses/Opportunities/Threats) analysis to determine how to take advantage of them to make your company successful.
- **Opportunities for Your Company**—Name opportunities forecasted and reported in various business and news magazines, journals, and programs. These can come from external sources and from inside your company. Anything that could help your company should be listed.

- **Threats to Your Company**—Name events that could threaten or harm your company from various business and news magazines, journals, and programs. Threats are internal and external. They threaten to reduce sales, profitability, growth or production.

New Strategic Plan

Finally, you are able to create your new plan. All of the previous analyses come together in this section to form a cohesive plan.

First, you will want to compare your strengths and weaknesses alongside your opportunities and threats. This is your SWOT analysis. Next, identify those key ingredients for success that can be maximized by your strengths and opportunities. Then, list your weaknesses and threats and how your strengths and opportunities can help to overcome them. Finally, you will want to pick out those areas you specifically want to improve on next year. You do not have to select everything. This will form the basis of your new plan.

- **New Company Objectives**—If you need new objectives, formulate them. These new objectives are based on your past objectives and what your SWOT analysis tells you what you need to do next year to improve your business.
- **Possible Strategies**—List as many possible strategies to improve your company as you can think of. Keep in mind that you want to maximize your strengths/opportunities and minimize your weaknesses/threats. Formulate strategies appropriately.
- **Chosen Strategies**—Choose the strategies that you feel will best create the desired outcome and meet the new objectives. Choose only those you can implement. Some may have to wait until next year. The most urgent needs should be addressed first.
- **Redefined Mission Statement**—If you need a new one after analysis, write one. Most likely, you will want to enhance the previous one.
- **Implementation of Chosen Strategies**—How will you implement the strategies? Make a listing of the ways

your strategies can be worked into your operations within your budget. If you are seeking more capital, note this.

- **Strategic Evaluation**—Determine how, over a period of time, you will measure and evaluate the success or failure of your chosen strategies. Once you determine a monthly, quarterly, or yearly evaluation timetable, stick to it.

Appendixes, Bibliography, and Indexes

This is an optional section to use if you generate supporting documents. If you have an elaborate strategic planning session, you may use this area.

SBA publication MP 21, Developing a Strategic Business Plan will also be of valued help as will EB06, Strategic Planning for Growing Businesses. The next chapter deals with other resources.

Continuously analyze, update, and revise the two to five year business strategy to incorporate changing circumstances, products, or economic forces. Do this through the Strategic Plan in the above table. This is very, very important. This is where businesses fail, and fail miserably. Recognize, Formulate, Implement, Evaluate. Even in times of success, you must continuously look over the horizon for future opportunities and threats, and behind your back at what your competitors are doing.

Continue to scan the environments—internal and external—for changes and patterns. This way, you can stay abreast of current trends and future trends as well. The best ways to do this, of course, are to order your competitors catalogs, products, or try their services on a periodic basis, in addition to keeping abreast of domestic and foreign events through news magazines, newspapers, and television. The next chapter contains a comprehensive list of resources, publications, and organizations to help grow and run your business.

Chapter 12

Resources, Resources, and More Resources

Where to Get Help, Information, and Supplies

This final chapter was written to inform you of the wide variety of sources of help, publications, services, software, government assistance, and supplies and suppliers. You will want to use this chapter's resources in conjunction with many of the other chapters in this book.

Fortunately, we live in the information age. This enables an individual like yourself to obtain more information on starting a business—and from a greater variety of sources—than anyone at any other time in our history. And the future looks even brighter. The key to a successful business idea, business plan, and business start-up is information. Only a strong foundation of information will allow you to grow into the company that your dreams first foresaw and your goals now envision.

This compendium of resources, agencies, and publications will be invaluable in your research and in the operation of your small business. We have included government agencies, individuals, and companies that have resources we feel might be of use to you. These sources can supply books, information, publications, supplies, advice, news, and statistics. Some, like the Small Business Administration, have publications for sale at little or moderate cost; others, like the Internal Revenue Service, send booklets free. Technical and expert advice and help is available from numerous government and private sector sources. Some of these have their own Web sites. Still, some of the listings are business suppliers who can provide forms, software, computers, et al.

Regardless of your business size or entity, many of these resources can be of great value to you. We especially like the Internet, because one site often links to other business sites. For example, the SBA site links to dozens of other government and private Web sites. We encourage the use of any and all free information on the Internet, because that simply saves you money. So it *is* worth your while to look into obtaining many of the resources offered and contacting the people, agencies, and companies listed. While this list is by no means exhaustive, it is a good guide of sources available to you.

We have broken the listings into categories depending on what resources they typically supply. Again, some categories will overlap.

Books and Booklets

- **Annual Rand McNally Commercial Atlas and Marketing Guide**—An annual digest of demographics on retail trade data, wholesale data, population estimates and projections; depicts target markets and every U.S. market. Invaluable for planning. Available at most libraries.

- **Business Building Ideas for Franchises and Small Business**—This booklet has ideas and suggestions on promoting your small business. The cost is $2.50.

  Med. Serif. Pilot Industries
  347 Fifth Ave.
  New York, NY 10016

- **Common Sense** by Art Williams—A financial booklet for individual investors. One of the best you will ever read on general finance; it is a great guide on how to save money to start your business. The cost is $2.45.

  Parklane Publishers Inc.
  PO Box 47105
  Doraville, GA 30362

- **The Essential Business Buyer's Guide** is a guide on purchasing anything associated with a business. It contains valuable information for the purchaser (most likely you) of your equipment and services. Check your local library or bookstore, or call Sourcebooks at 1-800-43-BRIGHT.

- **Franchise Opportunities Guide**—This is a guide from the IFA on franchises. Call 1-800-543-1038.

- **How to Select a Franchise**—This booklet and cassette contain information that will assist you in selecting your franchise. Cost is $10.00.

  > International Franchise Association (IFA)
  > 1350 New York Ave., NW
  > Suite 900
  > Washington, DC 20005-4709

- **How to Start and Run Your Home-Based Office** by Barry Z. Masser—A guide for the home-based business starter. Check your bookstore or library or call or write. (201) 592-2000.

  > Prentice Hall Career & Personal Development Div.
  > Prentice Hall Building
  > Englewood Cliffs, NJ 07632

- **Information USA** by Matthew Lesko—This is a great "little book" (actually, over 1000 pages) of addresses, names, numbers, and solid information on hundreds of topics. Invaluable. Available at bookstores and libraries.

- **Landex New Business Reference Guide**—This is a booklet published by the Syntex/IMS, Inc. It contains useful information on starting a business in individual metro areas. Write for a list of metro areas, and then get the booklet for your area.

  > Syntex/IMS, Inc
  > 8795 Ralston Rd, #112
  > Arvada, CO 80002

- **Mancuso's Small Business Basics** by Joseph R. Mancuso—A basic primer on starting small businesses by America's number one small business author. Call Sourcebooks at 1-800-43-BRIGHT.

- **Small Business Handbook** by Irving Burstiner—An excellent book for the first timer. Ask your librarian for a copy, or call or write to Prentice Hall Press to see if it is still in stock. See entry for *How to Start and Run Your Home-Based Office* for phone number and address.

- **Start Smart Your Home Based Business** by Bernadette Tiernan—A guide for the home-based business with information relevant to those specific start-ups. Check your bookstore or library or write the publisher, Macmillan.

  Macmillan
  1633 Broadway
  New York, NY 10019

- **Streetwise Small Business Start-Up** by Bob Adams— This book has loads of information on start-ups, from a master of small business, Bob Adams. Check your library or bookstore, or call: 1-800-872-5627. Also see their Web site at *www.adamsmedia.com.*

- **Your First Business Plan** by Joseph Covello and Brian Hazelgren—This sourcebook is a great book on writing a business plan. The book is available in bookstores, or call the publisher for a copy while you write your plan. Call: 1-800-43-BRIGHT.

Government Sources

- **Consumer Information Center**—Provides a catalog of free or cheap consumer federal publications. Some can aid your small business.
  CIC
  PO Box 100
  Pueblo, CO 81002

- **Copyrights**—These protect written documents against exploitation. If you produce written materials, art works, or software programs, you will need this information. Write:

  Register of Copyrights
  Library of Congress
  Washington, DC 20559-6000
  (202) 707-3000

- **Department of Commerce**—The commerce department has a Business Assistance Center and offers information.

- **Department of Labor**—Has publications on compliance with labor laws. Call (202) 219-9148 or write;

  Department of Labor
  200 Constitution Ave., NW
  Washington, DC 20210

- **Federal Trade Commission**—This organization has over one hundred free publications on consumer and business topics including the Consumer's Guide to Buying a Franchise.

  Public Reference
  Federal Trade Commission
  Washington, DC 20580

- **Government Auctions** are excellent ways to get furniture and equipment. Local and federal agencies hold auctions, check your local newspaper for information.

- **Internal Revenue Service**—The IRS has literally dozens of publications you can get. The best are the Small Business Tax Kit and Publication 334 Tax Guide for Small Business. Call (800) 829-3676 or visit the Web site *www.irs.ustreas.gov.* The IRS also offers local services like tax seminars and aid programs. Write: IRS, Washington, DC 20224.

- **Library**—Of course, you say. But the library is an excellent source of *free* resources and publications. The libraran will also be able to assist you in your searches. Your local library should have a business section that will contain guides to such things as trade associations, other companies, services, government information, statistical data, and phone books from other parts of the country.

- **Local Government**—Your local county or city government will likely have an economic development office where local assistance and certain SBA loans can be obtained. Most cities will have local loan, grant, or tax abatement programs such as the Urban Enterprise Zone initiatives.

- **Minority Business Development Agency**—This is the only Federal agency created to encourage minority ownership of small businesses. It coordinates federal programs, collects information and dispenses it, and funds training assistance for minorities at nine regional sites in Atlanta, Miami, Chicago, Dallas, New York, Boston, Philadelphia, San Francisco, and Los Angeles. For further information, call (202) 482-4547 or visit the MBDA Web site at *www.doc.gov/agencies/mbda/index.html.*

- **Small Business Administration**—The SBA is specifically geared toward encouraging small business growth and will provide you with most of your information, at least initially. The SBA has publications, videos, software, programs, loans, and Web sites. The publications, software, and videos are listed in the appendix. The *SBA's Small Business Development Centers* are located in every state and provide management assistance to current and potential small business owners. Its *Business Information Centers* are government/private ventures providing high-tech software and an array of counseling services and training to small businesses. *SBA field offices* are in every major city as are *Service Corps Of Retired Executive Centers,* which provides small business owners assistance from retired executives and businesspeople. See your state requirements for locations. The SBA National Ombudsman is at (312) 353-0880. Call the SBA Answer Desk at 1-800-8-ASK-SBA or visit the

SBA Web site at *www.sbaonline.sba.gov*. The address is:

SBA
409 Third Street NW
Washington, DC 20416

To obtain a list of SBA publications, write for the Resource Directory for Small Business Management:

SBA
PO BOX 46521
Denver, CO 80201

- **State Governments**—Like local governments, states often have their own economic development departments or departments of commerce. These can be treasure troves of booklets, pamphlets, and other information on starting small businesses. Check your state section in your phone book.

- **Superintendent of Documents**—This office handles Federal documents and publications. You can order a variety of things. Ask for a list of publications. Caution—the material may be slow to arrive.

    Superintendent of Documents
    U.S. Government Printing Office
    941 N Capitol St. NE
    Washington, DC 20402-9328

- **Trademarks and Patents**—To protect your trademark on your product or service, contact your state trademark agency and also the Federal government, which registers the trademark before the state does. Request the publication *Basic Facts about Registering a Trademark*. Cost is $4.00. To protect a patent, you must register with the Federal government. Request the booklet *General Information Concerning Patents*. Cost is $2.25. Write for patent and trademark information at:

    U.S. Commissioner of Patents and Trademarks
    Washington, DC 20231
    Phone: 1-800-786-9199

- **U.S. Government Bookstore**—These are in several major cities and contain publications from the government available to the public for sale.

Internet

- **Business Advisor Site**—This site will link you with all government Web sites and has a host of its own information. It is located at *www.business.gov.*

- **Entrepreneurial Edge Magazine**—*www.edgeonline.com* is a magazine for small business entrepreneurs with interviews, articles, and links to other great business resources, including the smallbiznet site.

- **Fed Stats**—*www.fedstats.com.* has a listing of government agencies that have stats on everything from the economy to businesses to the population—great site.

- **GTE SuperPages**—*www.superpages.GTE.net* is a directory assistance yellow pages for the Internet and costs $25.00 per month to get your business listed in it. This might bring in business and is relatively inexpensive.

- **Government Information Exchange**—*www.info.gov.* GIX is a Web site with some great government information and links to other sites.

- **Institute of Management and Administration**—*www.ioma.com* is a Web site linking you to over six hundred other business sites on the Internet. The site itself has a newsletter listing, a business directory, and discussion groups. IOMA publishes many of the newsletters. You might want to check this out to see if any pertain to you.

- **NASIRE**—*www.nasire.org.* This site contains links to every state Web site. It is a great place to surf for individual state information.

- **The Small Business Connection**—This site points to other Web sites and contains information on a Wayne State University program to help you start a small business. Fifty sites across the nation provide small business seminars. It is located at. *www.mcs.net/jkleb/index.html*

- Smartbiz—*www.smartbiz.com.* SmartBiz is a site devoted to providing lists and links to free resources for small businesses, such as publications, catalogs, and information.

Media

- **Bruce Williams**—Talknet Radio Program—This radio program is heard nightly on talk radio stations around the country. Mr. Williams often provides information and assistance to people starting businesses. Prepare your questions and problems in advance, and then call. The phone number is 1-800-825-5638, call between 7-10 pm EST, Monday thru Friday.

- **CNBC**—This network provides a host of business shows, many with small business topics. Especially useful is its morning line-up.

- **Local Broadcasting**—Many network television affiliates have business shows, especially during the noon hour or noon news. These might be sources of information or ways to promote your business (as a guest). Most talk radio stations have local programs, many business related. Check your local dials.

- **Nightly Business Report on PBS**—This program provides an overview of the day's business and financial news. Some of it directly pertains to small businesses.

Organizations and Groups

- **American Association of Franchisees and Dealers**—This group is a franchise organization that provides information, benefits, publications, and assistance to potential franchisees. Call 1-800-733-9858, visit their Web site at *www.aafd.org,* or write:

  AAFD
  PO Box 81887
  San Diego, CA 92138-1887

- **American Entrepreneur Association**—This is a group dedicated to providing benefits, information, and assistance to entrepreneurs. It publishes **Entrepreneur** and **Business Start-Ups** magazines (see appropriate section). For information, Call (714)-261-2325, visit the Web site at *www.entreprenuermag.com,* or write:

  AEA
  2392 Morse Ave.
  Irvine, CA 92714

- **American Society of Women Entrepreneurs**—The ASWE promotes women-owned businesses and lobbies on their behalf, while also providing access to publications and networking opportunities. Its Web site is at *www.aswe.org.* For more information, phone 1-888-669-2793 or write:

  ASWE
  2121 Precinct Rd, Suite 240
  Hurst, TX 76054

- **American Success Institute**—The ASI helps people starting businesses through a collection of resources and publications devoted to small and growing businesses. For more information, check out its Web site at *www.success.org,* phone 1-800-585-1300 or write:

  ASI
  5 N. Main Street
  Nantick, MA 01760

- **Better Business Bureau**—These bureaus are in all cities across the nation. The purpose is self-regulation and grievance redress. By joining, you receive the satisfaction that the BBB on your front counter brings. Call your local BBB for information on joining. It also has an online program. Call (703) 247-3667 or check out the BBB Web site *www.bbbonline.org.*

- **Chamber Of Commerce**—Most Chambers are made up of small businesses just like you. That's the backbone. Chambers provide members with information, networking, and business opportunities. The Chamber will work for your local business area. Membership is a good idea.

- **Direct Marketing Association**—This is a mail-order association that you can join if you plan mail-order sales.

  DMA

  6 East 43d Street

  New York, NY 10017

- **International Franchise Association**—This is similar to the AAFD and will provide information, booklets, and benefits to members. It puts out a publication called Franchise World—a good place to start your franchise research. Call (202) 628-8000, visit their Web site at www.franchise.org or write:

  IFA

  1350 New York Ave., NW Suite 900

  Washington, DC 20005-4709

- **Liberty Tree**—A group that puts out a catalog with libertarian and free market publications. Many relate to small businesses. To get a catalog, write:

  Liberty Tree

  134 Ninety-Eighth Ave.

  Oakland, CA 94603

- **National Association for the Self-Employed**—This group publishes two magazines for small business owners, including Self-Employed America, and provides information and benefits for members who are usually small business owners. Write:

  NASE

  2121 Precinct Line Rd

  Hurst, TX 76054

- **National Association of Women Business Owners**—This group lobbies for women's businesses and has information and services. Call (301)608-2590 or write:

  National Association of Women Business Owners
  1377 K Street NW
  Suite 637
  Washington, DC 20005

- **National Federation of Independent Businesses**—This group of 600,000 businesses is a lobbying organization for small businesses. It recently helped score some important tax and law victories for small businesses. Call them at 615-872-5800 or 1-800-NFIB-NOW, visit their Web site at *www.nfibonline.com* or write to:

  NFIB
  53 Century Blvd
  Suite 300
  Nashville, TN 37214

- **The New Careers Center (Publisher)**—This company produces a catalog with a variety of great small business publications. Here is a sample list of their titles:
  - *How to Form Your Own Corporation Without a Lawyer*
  - *Guerrilla Financing: Alternative Techniques to Finance Any Small Business*
  - *Working Solo Sourcebook: Essential Resources for Independent Entrepreneurs*
  - *Ecopreneuring*
  - *The Work-At-Home Sourcebook*
  - *The Complete Work-At-Home Companion*
  - *Home Business 101*
  - *Free Money from the Federal Government for Small Businesses And Entrepreneurs*
  - *Small Time Operator*
  - *The Start Up Guide: A One Year Plan for Entrepreneurs*
  - *Starting and Operating a Business in…(each state has a guide)*
  - *Marketing for the Home-Based Business*
  - *The Complete Small Business Loan Kit*

This is just a sampling of the great books for small business owners. We recommend ordering their catalog.

Write:

New Careers Center
1515 23rd Street
Box 339-AT
Boulder, CO 80306

- **SOHO America Association**—This group represents SOHO businesses as an organization and provides networking, news and stories, benefits such as discount travel and health insurance, as well as keeping tabs on the state of SOHO businesses. Call 1-800-495-SOHO for more information or e-mail the group at *info@soho.org*.

Publications

- **Business Start-Ups**—This magazine presents ideas for new and potential entrepreneurs. It usually has four or five feature articles and has several departments with information and news relevant to all small businesses. A subscription is $9.95/year. Call 1-800-274-8333 or visit their Web site at *www.entrepreneurmag.com*.

- **Extra Income**—This magazine is geared at small and home-based businesses. Like its title suggests, it concentrates on businesses that are part-time or extracurricular in nature. It contains articles, information, and advertising. A subscription is $11.95. Write:

Business Concepts
734 Monte Drive
Santa Barbara, CA 93110

- **Income Opportunities**—This magazines calls itself the original small business/home office magazine. It usually contains profiles of small businesses, opportunity listings, small business news, small business articles and other relevant information. The Cost is $17.89. Call or visit their Web site *www.incomeops.com*. Write:

Income Opportunities
PO Box 55206
Boulder, CO 80322

- **INC**—This magazine is for somewhat larger companies and even corporations, but INC usually has a great deal of small business news and articles. A recent issue contained a profile of the small business world, its economy, and scope. It is available at news stands.

- **Nation's Business**—A U.S. Chamber of Commerce publication contains dozens of articles and departments each month on issues pertaining to truly small businesses. It often has news on legal and regulatory updates. This is a good publication to subscribe to. A subscription is $22.00/year. Call 1-800-638-6582.

- **Wall Street Journal, Business Week, Fortune, Forbes, Barrons, USA TODAY**—These heavy hitters cover the corporate and small business worlds. You should browse through them now and then to see if there is anything that might be of use to you. They are a great way to keep abreast of industry trends and the economy as a whole.

Services

- **Business Start-Up Guides**—Again, the American Entrepreneurial Association produces these guides that contain information on starting over one hundred different types of businesses. Included are start-up costs, capital raising ideas, market analysis, and other financial and management information. Call 1-800-421-2300 for a catalog. Most are around $75.00.

- **CCH, Inc.**—This company provides publications and information on everything from marketing to employees to business start-ups to aspiring small business owners. Its Web site at *www.toolkit.cch.com* is excellent; many free resources are located here. For more information, call (847) 267-2196 or write:

CCH, Inc.
2700 Lake Cook Rd
Riverwoods, IL 60015

- **Charles Schwabb**—For personal finance, you might want to check out a discount brokerage like Schwabb.

- **The Company Corporation**—This company will incorporate you, for a fee, in any of the states. Prices start at $45.00 plus filing fees. Call 1-800-542-2677 or visit the Web site at *www.incorporate.com* for more information. Write:

    Company Corporation
    1313 N. Market Street
    Wilmington, DE 19801-1151

- **Home Business Opportunity Library**—A collection of publications/audio/video tapes on starting small home-based businesses. Call 1-800-858-4783 for more information.

- **K-Mart Supplier Diversity Department**—This is a program by K-Mart that enables a review of your product for possible placement in K-Mart stores. Write:

    K-Mart Supplier Diversity Department
    3100 West 16 Mile Road
    Troy, MI 48084

- **Lab Safety Supply, Inc.**—Has a catalog of safety supplies and has a listing of labor, environmental, food, and transportation regulation manuals. Call 1-800-356-0783 for a catalog.

- **Merchant's Choice Card Services**—Credit card accepting systems. Call 1-800-687-2776 for information.

- **National Business Library Start-Up Guides**—These guides will help you start one of over sixty businesses. These blueprints contain a plethora of stats, strategies, and information for about $40 each. Call 1-800-947-7724 for more information or write:

    National Business Library
    PO Box 928
    Los Olivos, CA 93441

- **Nation's Business Magazine**—That's right, this magazine has a plethora of publications, software, and videos for sale. The sources are varied, but the magazine provides one location for you to "shop." Check out an issue.

- **Pitney Bowes**—Mailing and information systems. Check your local yellow pages.

Suppliers

- **American Business Lists**—A company supplying mailing lists of nine million businesses and seventy-eight million individuals. Call (402) 331-7169 for information.

- **Dome Publishing**—This company publishes book-keeping, payroll, and budget books and computer software. You can buy them at offices supply stores or write for a catalog:

  Dome Publishing
  10 New England Way
  Warwick, RI 02887-9976

- **NEBS, Inc.**—This company produces business forms for advertising, bidding, billing, check writing, document-ing, labeling, mailing, organizing, and selling. Write them for a catalog, although as a new business they may mail you one eventually anyway. You can also call 1-800-367-6327.

  NEBS, Inc.
  500 Main Street
  Groton, MA 01471

- **Office Depot, Staples, Office Max, Best Buy**—These are national chain business and computer/software supply stores. They often beat local competitors on prices. The first three carry an array of supplies, books, computers, furniture, and office/stationary products. The later has a line of business software and computers.

- **Reliable**—Sells office equipment through mail order. Write for a catalog:

    Reliable
    1001 Van Buren Street
    Chicago, IL 60607

- **Selective Software**—A company that sells dozens of informative, inexpensive, and useful software programs for business. From accounting to personnel to planning. Write for a catalog:

    Selective Software
    3004 Mission Street
    Santa Cruz, CA 95060

- **Software**—The industry standard has become Windows® based programs. These include Word Perfect and Microsoft Word for word processing, Lotus and Excel for spreadsheets, and Money for finance management; as well as Quickbooks Pro, Peachtree Accounting, Best Ware's M.Y.O.B. for accounting and billing. Database programs include FoxPro and Access. All are available at software stores and chains.

- **World's Easiest Software**—This is available at many office supply or software stores. It has software to make business cards, certificates, promotion materials, and other essential business documents. Visit the Web site at *www.easiest.com.*

In addition, there are literally hundreds and thousands of suppliers of *specific* items for businesses, as well as hundreds of industry specific publications and service providers. To check for suppliers for equipment unique to your business, we suggest you consult the yellow pages of your phone book *and* those of larger cities such as Chicago, New York, Los Angeles, Detroit, Atlanta, Boston, San Francisco, etc. Many "industry" magazines (those relating to your specific business) have excellent advertising sections where suppliers advertise their companies and products.

Another excellent place to obtain product/supplier information is trade shows. These are held all over the country and cover literally all businesses. Here, related suppliers, dealers, and manufacturers gather under one roof to display their products and services. You can obtain information directly from company representatives at the trade show or convention. Not only is it a good way to see products up close and in person, but it is a great way to make contacts inside the supplier company.

This list is by no means exhaustive. Many trade journals and academic journals can be consulted as can colleges (business and economics professors), government publications and agencies, and private think tanks.

Part II

State Requirements

Introduction

This part of the book lists state offices and addresses, statistics, and requirements. We have updated not only the start-up information for each state but have also included more sources of help within each state. These sources include Business Investment Centers, Minority Business Development Agencies, Web sites and first stop business locations. Not all states have the same amount or quality of sources, but each at least has a Small Business Development Center and a Web site.

The Secretary of State generally handles incorporations; revenue handles state sales tax numbers, use numbers, and exempt numbers. That office can send you the necessary forms and may answer some questions you have. Still, be sure to ask a lawyer, accountant, and/or one of the other sources listed above for thorough consultation. Utilizing the SBA and its resources is usually a good bet.

We surveyed the Secretaries of State and the Revenue Offices of all fifty states and the District of Columbia. They provided us with forms, information, and answered questionnaires we mailed. The information is correct for 1997 unless indicated. *IMPORTANT:* Relying on outdated information can cause you to be fined for improper action by the state. Therefore, you should use this as a *guide only*, not as the definitive truth. Any misprints or deletions are unintentional, and you use the information without first consulting a lawyer at your own risk. Again, the facts are as complete as we could make them with the information supplied to us by the states as of August 1997. Any new state laws or regulations should be noted by you and your lawyer, and followed.

You will immediately note that some information for certain states is more complete than for other states. This is because many of the states also sent booklets or folios explaining their state's regulations and laws. You will also note those states that seemed to have gone out of their way to send extra information to us.

Generally, you will need to secure a Federal Identification Number, register your business entity with your state and local officials, and obtain state tax registration. Along the way, you may have to apply for licenses or other permits as well. But that is all the actual start-up is generally composed of. Within each registration phase might be other phases.

If you are going to start a sole proprietorship or a general partnership, you generally just need to register with your county official, usually the clerk or recorder. Sometimes you will need a city business license as well. Call to find out. There may also be zoning restrictions or requirements to consider.

For corporations and limited liability companies, the process is more involved. Here is a sample of the steps one might take to incorporate in Indiana.

Sample Indiana Incorporation Steps

Federal Employer ID Number (Tax ID)
- File SS-4 Federal Employer Identification Number.

State Business Registration
- File a Name Reservation Form.
- File the Articles of Incorporation.
- File Trade Name Registration.

Local Business Registration
- Register with the County Recorder.

State Tax Registration
- File form BT-1 for withholding tax, sales and use tax and to get a tax exempt ID number.

Licenses
- While going through the process obtain any and all licenses and permits you will need. A lawyer is a good one to talk to if you think you need these.

As you can see in this example, six forms were filed. The total cost would be around $135.00, excluding any fees for a lawyer or an accountant. The process will take a few weeks, but you can always expedite things over the phone. Many states offer one or two day expedited services for higher fees. If you are in a hurry, this might be for you. State fees vary, and do not forget, you can form a corporation in states like Nevada or Delaware even if you do not live there.

Many states strongly suggest using a lawyer when you incorporate, but again, that is up to you. We also think it is a good idea to use a lawyer for all aspects of incorporation, especially when filing for foreign corporation, limited liability company, or limited partnership status in another state. This is merely to protect you from legal, tax, and regulatory problems. A foreign corporation, limited liability company, or limited partnership is an entity formed in another state under different laws (albeit very similar laws). Thus, if you are an Indiana corporation and set up a shop or do business in Ohio, you must register in Ohio as a foreign corporation. The regulations here can be tricky, so get legal help first. Note, too, that if your business plan calls for stores or transactions across state lines, *plan your filing of requirements early* so that when the time comes, you can register as a foreign corporation without delay. Also, foreign corporations are often asked to obtain certificates of existence or good standing from their original state when filing foreign corporation forms.

Most states also require that certain entities have Company, Corporation, Incorporated, Limited Liability Company, or Limited Partnership as part of the name (in most the abbreviations of the words are suitable). Your state will send information on this, but it is a good idea to plan on using one of the words or an abbreviation.

Assumed or fictitious names are those used generally by partnerships or sole proprietors when their business name is different from their entity name. Sometimes companies use a Doing Business As (DBA) statement to use a name different from their actual name.

Other start-up considerations are annual reports for corporations, some partnerships, and limited liability companies; securities regulations for corporations; employment commissions and agencies; and regulatory boards and other requirements such as Uniform Commercial Code filings. This is where a lawyer or your state offices can provide more detailed information. This book is not designed to cover everything concerning every business or industry. Still, you do not want to get bogged down *after* you have started business because you did not file all of the proper papers with the proper agencies or do not have all the right permits.

We have included two sample letters that you can use as guides for obtaining information from the Secretary of State and/or the State

Revenue Office. They are guides only, and your letters should be unique and in your own words. However, you want to state your purpose and what information/services you desire. Many states appreciate a self-addressed 9x12 envelope. Since you do not know how much the return mail will cost, omit postage.

Do, however, write the state for information beforehand. The information provided below is intended to guide you and open your mind to the complexity of starting a business. for further information on any of the aspects below, write to the applicable state.

Following the letters is a worksheet (Business Checklist) to help you keep the process in order. Additionally, appendix C contains a worksheet designed to help you research the start-up needs and requirements for your small business. Remember to use our information, as well as any you glean from the state sources listed below.

Letter One

Date

Your Address

Secretary of State
Capitol Bldg
Capital City, Anystate 00000

To Whom It May Concern:

I am in the process of researching my small business start-up and would like any information you may have.

Could you please send me information on the following type of business entities: (Pick only those you need information on)

1. Sole Proprietors
2. Partnerships
3. Corporations
4. Limited Liability Company
5. Limited Liability Partnership

I need information relating to fees, procedures, regulations, and rules. In addition, any forms or publications your office has will be greatly appreciated.

Thank you for your time and consideration. I look forward to your reply.

Sincerely,

Your Name

Letter Two:

Date

Your Address

Department of Revenue
A Street
Capital City, Anystate 00000

To Whom It May Concern:

Please send to me the proper forms and documentation to obtain a sales tax and/or use number, and for other applicable state taxes such as income withholding.

In addition, any additional tax information concerning small businesses in Anystate will be greatly appreciated. I intend to use this information with my lawyer and/or accountant while I go through the process of starting my business.

Thank you for your time and consideration. I look forward to your reply.

Sincerely,

Your Name

Worksheet: Business Checklist

Business Entity:

☐ Sole Proprietorship
☐ General Partnership
☐ Limited Partnership
☐ Limited Liability Company
☐ Limited Liability Partnership
☐ Corporation
☐ S-Corporation

Checklist Steps:

☐ Federal EIN—Form SS-4: Federal Level

☐ Entity Name Reservation: State Level
Form(s):_____

☐ Tax Registration
Sales, Use, Withholding, Excise, Other:_____
Form(s):_____
Form(s):_____

☐ Business Registration: State Level
Form(s):_____

☐ Trade Name Registration: State Level
Form(s):_____

☐ Business Registration: Local/County Level
Licenses/Form(s):_____

☐ State/Local Licensing or Permits
Agency:_____
Phone Number:_____
Form(s):_____

Agency:_____

Phone Number:_____

Form(s):_____

☐ **Workers Compensation Insurance/Other Employment Necessities**

Agency:_____

Phone Number:_____

Form(s):_____

Agency:_____

Phone Number:_____

Form(s):_____

☐ **Assumed or Fictitious Name Registration/Doing Business As Registration**

Form(s):_____

☐ **Trademark, Copyright or Patent: Federal Level and Certain States (TM)**

Type Needed (If any):_____

_____

_____

State Requirements

Alabama

Office of the Sect of State
Attn: Corporate Section
PO Box 5616
Montgomery, AL 36103
(334) 242-5324

Central Registration Unit
PO Box 327100
Montgomery, AL 36132
(334) 242-1170

Start-Up Requirements

Business Registration Requirements

Incorporation:
- You must first obtain a Certificate of Name Reservation from the Corporations Section of the Secretary of State. Cost: $10.00, collected by the Judge of Probate.
- File the Articles of Incorporation and deposit in the office of the Judge of Probate in the county the corporation's registered office is located. File the original and two copies. Cost: $35.00 to the Judge of Probate, plus $50.00 to the Secretary of State, which includes a $40.00 filing fee and the $10.00 fee for the name reservation.

Limited Liability Company:
- Articles of Organization are filed with the Office of Judge of Probate in your county. Cost: $75.00.
- File the Report of Domestic LLC with the Secretary of State. Cost: $5.00. File within thirty days of the Articles.

Limited Liability Partnership:
- File a Limited Liability Partnership Registration. Cost: $75.00

Limited Partnership:
- File the Limited Liability Partnership Registration. Cost: $35.00 to Judge of Probate in your county, $40.00 to Secretary of State.

Sole Proprietor and General Partnership:
- Check with your County Recorder or local officials.

Foreign Entities:
- Corporations, limited liability companies, limited partnerships and other businesses must file forms to transact business in the state. The fees and forms vary. They can be obtained from the Secretary of State's address above.

Tax Registration Requirements

Sales and Withholding Tax:
- File the Combined Registration Form (COM-101). This form also registers you for other state taxes. Cost: None listed. The sales tax rate is 4%.

In-State Help and Information
- The Business Information Center (BIC) phone number was not listed. Call (202) 205-6665 to see if Alabama has set one up yet.
- SBA Office: Birmingham, Phone: (205) 731-1344.
- Small Business Development Center, University of Alabama, Birmingham. Phone: (205) 934-7260.
- Call 1-800-8-ASK-SBA for SCORE locations.
- Securities Information: Securities Commission, Phone: (334) 242-2984.
- E-mail: *alabiz@alainc.net*

Notes: For incorporations, the State recommends prior contact with the Judge of Probate in the corporation's county, because some counties charge a recording fee. The inclusion of a "Judge of Probate" payment in many entity elections tells us that you should take care to file the right forms and requirements. The Department of Revenue can send you a handy Alabama Business Taxes booklet.

Source: Secretary of State's Office and Department of Revenue

Alaska

Dept of Commerce and Econ. Dev.
Division of Corporations
PO Box 110808
Juneau, AK 99811-0808
(907) 465-2530

Dept of Revenue
PO Box 110420
Juneau, AK 99811-0420
(907) 465-2375

Start-Up Requirements

Business Registration Requirements

Incorporation:
- File the Application for Reservation of Name. Cost: $25.00
- File the Articles of Incorporation. Cost: $150.00. Note, the total cost is $250.00 but that includes the Biennial Tax listed below.
- File the Application for Registration of Name. Cost: $25.00 (Must be renewed each year).
- The Biennial Corporation Tax is due at the time of incorporation. Cost: $100.00
- File a Statement of SIC code. Cost: None
- File an Alaska Business License Application. Cost: $50.00 to $75.00

Limited Liability Company:
- File the Application for Reservation of Name. Cost: $25.00 (Might be optional)
- File the Articles of Organization. Cost: $250.00
- File the Application for Registration of Name. Cost: $25.00 (Must be renewed each year).
- You may also need to file an Alaska Business License Application. Cost: $50.00 to $75.00

Limited Partnership:
- File the Application for Reservation of Name. Cost: $25.00 (Might be optional)
- File the Application for Registration of Name. Cost: $25.00 (must be renewed each year).
- File a Certificate of Limited Partnership. Cost: $150.00
- File an Alaska Business License Application. Cost: $50.00 to $75.00

Sole Proprietor and General Partnership:
- File an Alaska Business License Application. Cost: $50.00 to $75.00
- Check with local officials on other licenses or permits.

Foreign Entities:
- Corporations, limited liability companies, limited partnerships and other businesses must file forms to transact business in the state. The fees and forms vary. They can be obtained from the Secretary of State's address above.

Tax Registration Requirements

Sales and Withholding Tax:

- Alaska has no state sales tax, use tax, or personal income taxes. Some cities and local governments do have taxes, however. Check your city or borough. Excise taxes are levied on fuel, tobacco, alcohol and fishing.

In-State Help and Information

- The Business Information Center (BIC) phone number was not listed. Call (202) 205-6665 to see if Alaska has set one up yet.
- SBA Office: Anchorage, Phone: (907) 271-4022.
- Small Business Development Center, University of Alaska/Anchorage. Phone: (907) 274-7232.
- Call 1-800-8-ASK-SBA for SCORE locations.
- Securities Information: Division of Banking, Phone: (907) 465-2521.
- State Web site: *www.state.ak.us.*

Notes: Write to the address above for a complete set of forms and instructions. A plethora of information and forms will be sent to you and they are very helpful. With virtually no taxation except at the corporate level, this is a low "requirement" state.

Source: Department of Commerce and Economic Development and The Department of Revenue

Arizona

Arizona Corporation Commission
1300 W. Washington
Phoenix, AZ 85007-2929
(602) 542-3135
(800) 345-5819 (Arizona residents only)

Dept of Revenue
1600 W Monroe
Phoenix, AZ 85007-2650
(602) 542-2076

or

400 W. Congress
Tucson, AZ 58701-1347
(520) 628-6560

Start-Up Requirements

Business Registration Requirements

Incorporation:

- Reserve a name with the Arizona Corporation Commission. Cost: $10.00
- File one original and one copy of the Articles of Incorporation. Cost: $60.00
- File a Certificate of Disclosure. Cost: None listed.
- After filing the articles, the articles publish for three consecutive days in a newspaper in your county, and file an affidavit of that publication with the Arizona Corporation Commission.

Limited Liability Company and Limited Liability Partnership:

- Contact the Arizona Corporation Commission for information.

Limited Partnership: (1994 information)
- Reserve a name with the Arizona Corporation Commission. Cost: $10.00
- Next, execute a certificate of limited partnership by filing it with the Secretary of State. List your name, addresses, cash and statement of property, and other requirements listed in the Arizona Limited Partnerships publication, pages 6 and 7. Cost: $10.00, plus $3.00 per page.

Sole Proprietor and General Partnership:
- Check with your local and county governments for licensing information.

Foreign Entities:
- Corporations, limited liability companies, limited partnerships, and other businesses must file forms to transact business in the state. The fees and forms vary. They can be obtained from the Arizona Corporation Commission's address above.

Tax Registration Requirements

Transaction Privilege Tax and Withholding:
- File the Arizona Joint Tax Application form ADOR50-4002, which also registers you for other taxes. Cost: $12.00 fee for each business location.

In-State Help and Information
- The Business Information Center (BIC) phone number was not listed. Call (202) 205-6665 to see if Arizona has set one up yet.
- SBA Office: Phoenix, Phone: (602) 640-2316.
- Small Business Development Center, Maricopa County Community College, Tempe. Phone: (602) 731-8202.
- Call 1-800-8-ASK-SBA for SCORE locations.
- Business Assistance Centers: Phoenix, Phone: (602) 280-1480 and Tucson, Phone: (520) 628-6690.
- Securities Information: Corporation Commission, Securities Division, Phone: (602) 542-4242.
- State Web site: *www.state.az.us*

Notes: Ask for the Arizona Business Guide from the Department of Revenue. The Business Assistance Centers offer information and resources for start-up businesses as well as The Small Business Book about starting an Arizona business.

Source: Secretary of State's Office and Department of Revenue

Arkansas

Secretary of State
Off of the Sect of State
State Capitol
Little Rock, AR 72201-1094
(501) 371-1010

Revenue Division
Dept of Finance and Admin
PO Box 1272
Little Rock, AR 72203
(501) 682-7000

Start-Up Requirements

Business Registration Requirements

Incorporation:
- File the Application for Reservation of Corporate Name. Cost: $25.00
- File the Application for Registration of Corporate Name. Cost: $50.00

- File duplicate Articles of Incorporation with the Secretary of State. Cost: $50.00
- The Corporate Franchise Tax—form FT-11- is due on June 1 of the year following the year of incorporation. (Strongly suggest you consult a lawyer on this.) However, *you must file the Corporate Franchise Tax form at the time of incorporation in order to receive the corporate franchise tax reporting form.* Cost: The amount will vary based on your assets and stock.
- S-corporations must file an Arkansas AR-1103 form.

Limited Liability Company:
- File the Application for Reservation of Limited Liability Company Name. Cost: $25.00
- File the Articles of Organization. Cost: $50.00

Limited Liability Partnership:
- File the Application for Registration of Limited Liability Partnership. Cost: $50.00

Limited Liability Limited Partnership:
- File the Application for Registration of Limited Liability Limited Partnership. Cost: $50.00

Limited Partnership:
- File a Certificate of Limited Partnership, plus one copy, with the Secretary of State. The form needs to be notarized. Cost: $50.00

Sole Proprietor and General Partnership:
- Check your County Recorder and local agencies for requirements.

Foreign Entities:
- Corporations, limited liability companies, limited partnerships, and other businesses must file forms to transact business in the state. The fees and forms vary. They can be obtained from the Secretary of State's address above.

Tax Registration Requirements

Sales Tax:
- File an Application for Permit to register for the sales tax permit. Cost: $50.00

Withholding:
- File form AR4ER Withholding Registration. Cost: None listed

In-State Help and Information
- The Business Information Center (BIC) was not listed. Call (202) 205-6665 to see if Arkansas has set one up yet.
- SBA Office: Little Rock. Phone: (501) 324-5278.
- Small Business Development Center, University of Arkansas, Little Rock. Phone: (501) 324-9043.
- Call 1-800-8-ASK-SBA for SCORE locations.
- Securities Department (Stock). Phone: (501) 324-9260.
- State Web site: *www.state.ar.us*

Notes: The Secretary of State's Office will send you every form under the sun. Ask the Revenue Department for its Starting a New Business in Arkansas. Certain corporations will have to file their estimated quarterly State income tax liability through electronic funds transfer.

Source: Secretary of State's Office and Revenue Division, Department of Finance and Administration

California

Secretary of State
1500 11th Street
Sacramento, CA 95814
(916) 657-5448

State Board of Equalization
PO Box 942879
Sacramento, CA 94279-0090
1-800-400-7115

Start-Up Requirements

Business Registration Requirements

Incorporation:
- You may wish to reserve a proposed name. (Send to the attention of the Name Availability Unit). Cost: $10.00
- File the Articles of Incorporation with the Secretary of State and send it to the above address to the attention of Document Filing Support Unit, 1500 11th St, Sacramento, CA 95814. Cost: $100.00 for the Articles, but an additional $600 or $800 franchise tax must be submitted with your Articles.

Limited Liability Company:
- Reserve a Limited Liability Company name. Cost: $10.00
- File the Articles of Organization, Form LLC-1 with the SOS, LLC Unit, Box 944228, Sacramento CA 94244. Cost: $70.00
- File an Initial Statement of Information within ninety days. Cost: $10.00

Limited Liability Partnership:
- File the Registered Limited Liability Partnership Registration with the SOS, LLP Unit, PO Box 944228, Sacramento CA 94244. Cost: $70.00

Limited Partnership:
- Reserve a limited partnership name. Cost: $10.00
- File the Certificate of Limited Partnership (Form LP-1) with the SOS, Limited Partnership Division, PO Box 944225, Sacramento, CA 94244. Cost: $70.00

General Partnership:
- File a Statement of Partnership Authority, Form GP-1 with SOS General Partnership Unit, PO Box 944225, Sacramento CA 94244. Cost: $70.00
- Also check with the County Recorders and local government for further regulations.

Sole Proprietor:
- Check with the County Recorders and local government for further regulations.

Foreign Entities:
- Corporations, limited liability companies, limited partnerships, and other businesses must file forms to transact business in the state. The fees and forms vary. They can be obtained from the Secretary of State's address above.

Tax Registration Requirements

Sales Tax:
- You must obtain a sellers permit (for each business location) from your local Equalization Board. Write for a list of local Boards. Partners and sole proprietors will file form BOE-400-MIP (S1F) and Corporations/Limited Liability Companies file BOE-400-MCO (S1F). Contact your local Equalization Board for additional information.

Withholding Tax:
- File as a new employer with form DE-1. Cost: None listed.

In-State Help and Information
- The Business Information Centers (BICs) are in Chula Vista, Phone: (619) 482-6375; Los Angeles, Phone: (213) 251-7253; San Diego, Phone: (619) 557-7252.
- SBA Field Offices: Fresno, Phone (209) 487-5791; Glendale, Phone: (818) 552-3210; Sacramento, Phone: (916) 498-6410; San Diego, Phone: (169) 557-7252; Santa Ana, Phone: (714) 550-7420; San Francisco, Phone: (415) 744-2118.
- Small Business Development Center, California Trade and Commerce Agency, Sacramento. Phone: (916) 324-5061.
- Call 1-800-8-ASK-SBA for SCORE locations.
- Minority Business Development Agency locations: San Francisco, Phone: (415) 744-3001 and Los Angeles, Phone: (313) 613-1300.
- The One Stop Capital Shops are located at Glendale, Phone: (818) 552-3308 and Oakland, Phone: (510) 0620.
- Securities Information: Securities Division. Phone: (213) 736-2713.
- Web site: *www.boe.ca.gov* for the Board of Equalization.

Notes: Contact your local Equalization Board for sales tax rates in your area.

Source: Secretary of State and State Board of Equalization

Colorado

Secretary of State
Department of State
1560 Broadway, Suite 200
Denver, CO 80202
(303) 894-2251

Dept of Revenue
1375 Sherman St
Denver, CO 80261
(303) 323-2416

Start-Up Requirements

Business Registration Requirements

Incorporation:
- File the Articles of Incorporation with the Secretary of State. Cost: $50.00

Limited Liability Company:
- File the Articles of Organization. Cost: $50.00

Limited Liability Partnership:
- No information supplied.

Limited Partnership:
- File the Certificate of Limited Partnership for a Colorado Limited Partnership. Cost: $50.00

Sole Proprietor and General Partnership:
- Check with your County Recorder and city officials for their regulations.

Foreign Entities:
- Corporations, limited liability companies, limited partnerships, and other businesses must file forms to transact business in the state. The fees and forms vary. They can be obtained from the Secretary of State's address above.

Tax Registration Requirements

Sales and Withholding Tax:
- To obtain a license or number, fill out the Colorado Business Registration form, CR-100. Cost: Ranges from $12.00 to $20.00 depending on the time of the year and your trade name if necessary, plus a $50.00 tax deposit.

In-State Help and Information
- The Business Information Center (BIC) is in Denver, Phone: (303) 844-3986.
- SBA Office: Denver. Phone: (303) 844-0500.
- Small Business Development Center, Department of Business Development, Denver. Phone: (303) 892-3809.
- Colorado Business Assistance Center, Phone: (303) 592-5920.
- Call 1-800-8-ASK-SBA for SCORE locations.
- Securities Information: Department of Regulatory Agencies. Phone: (303) 894-2320.
- State Web site: *www.state.co.us.*

Notes: You will want to check on the name registration of your business, and as always, on possible state regulations of your industry, service, or profession. Be sure to double check the tax fees. The Colorado Department of Revenue sent us a Colorado Business Start Up Kit which will be invaluable to you. Specifically ask for it by calling (303) 232-2434.

Source: Secretary of State's Office and Department of Revenue

Connecticut

Secretary of State
State Capitol
Hartford, CT 06115
(203) 566-2739

Dept of Revenue Services
25 Sigourney Street
Hartford, CT 06106
1-800-382-9463
In State (806) 566-7120

Start-Up Requirements

Business Registration Requirements

Incorporation:
- File an Application for Reservation of Corporate Name. Cost: $30.00
- File the Certificate of Incorporation for a stock corporation and the Organization and First Report. Cost: $275.00 minimum depending on your shares of stock.
- Non-stock companies will only pay $65.00

Limited Liability Company:
- File an Application to Reserve a Limited Liability Company Name. Cost: $30.00
- File the Articles of Organization, including Appointment of Statutory Agent. Cost: $60.00

Limited Liability Partnership:
- File an Application to Reserve a Limited Liability Partnership Name. Cost: $30.00
- File a Certificate of Limited Liability Partnership. Cost: $60.00

Limited Partnership:
- File an Application for Reservation of Limited Partnership Name. Cost: $30.00

- File the Certificate of Limited Partnership and Appointment of Statutory Agent. Cost: $60.00

Sole Proprietor and General Partnership:
- Check your County Recorder or Town Clerk.

Foreign Entities:
- Corporations, limited liability companies, limited partnerships, and other businesses must file forms to transact business in the state. The fees and forms vary. They can be obtained from the Secretary of State's address above.

Tax Registration Requirements

Sales and Withholding Tax:
- File the Application for Tax Registration Number REG-1. This form also registers you for other state taxes. Cost: $20.00

In-State Help and Information
- The Business Information Center (BIC) phone number was not listed. Call (202) 205-6665 to see if Connecticut has set one up now.
- SBA Office: Hartford, Phone: (203) 240-4700.
- Small Business Development Center, University of Connecticut, Storrs. Phone: (203) 486-4135
- Call 1-800-8-ASK-SBA for SCORE locations.
- Securities Information: Securities and Business Investments Division. Phone: (860) 240-8299.
- State Web site: *www.state.ct.us*

Notes: The Secretary of State's Office strongly recommends "that an attorney and/or other competent advisors be consulted." A valuable form is Form 1033C-11/14 which lists various fees. The state is unable to provide assistance as to completion of forms or any other matters incidental to incorporation.

Source: Secretary of State's Office and Department of Revenue Services

Delaware

Secretary of State
Department of State
Townsend Bldg
Dover, DE 19901
(302) 739-3073

Division of Revenue
Dept of Finance
820 N French St
Wilmington, DE 19801
(302) 577-5800

Start-Up Requirements

Business Registration Requirements

Incorporation:
- Reserve a name by telephone. From within Delaware, call (900) 420-8042. Cost: $10.00 (You will need a Visa or Mastercard)
- File a Certificate of Incorporation in duplicate. Write for forms and information. Cost: $50.00 minimum based on shares and value of stock, plus any county fees and an annual franchise tax fee.

Limited Liability Company:
- Reserve a name by telephone. From within Delaware, call (900) 420-8042. Cost: $10.00 (You will need a Visa or Mastercard)
- File the Limited Liability Company Certificate of Formation. Cost: $70.00 plus annual renewal fees.

Limited Liability Partnership:
- Reserve a name by telephone. From within Delaware, call (900) 420-8042. Cost: $10.00 (You will need a Visa or Mastercard)
- File the Limited Liability Partnership Certificate of Application. Cost: $100.00 per partner plus annual renewal fees.

Limited Partnership:
- File a Certificate of Limited Partnership. Cost: $220.00, plus annual renewal fees.

Sole Proprietor and General Partnership:
- Check the County Recorder or Clerk. No information was sent to us.

Foreign Entities:
- Corporations, limited liability companies, limited partnerships, and other businesses must file forms to transact business in the state. The fees and forms vary. They can be obtained from the Secretary of State's address above.

Tax Registration Requirements

Sales and Withholding Tax:
- Delaware does not assess sales tax. There are, however, other taxes and licensing fees. File the Combined Registration Application to register for withholding taxes, a business license and other taxes. Cost: Varies.

In-State Help and Information
- The Business Information Center (BIC) is in Wilmington, Phone: (302) 831-1555.
- SBA Office: Wilmington, Phone: (302) 573-2694.
- Small Business Development Center, University of Delaware, Newark. Phone: (302) 831-2747.
- Call 1-800-8-ASK-SBA for SCORE locations.
- Securities Information: Division of Securities. Phone: (302) 577-2515.
- State Web site: *www.state.de.us*

Notes: There are over 230,000 companies incorporated in Delaware, and many are small businesses. Every Delaware corporation must have a registered agent in Delaware. A list is given in the booklet the Secretary of State will send you, which is a fantastic start-up guide. Annual reports and franchise taxes are due each year. Delaware can offer many things to a business, and is considered "pro-business." You may need to file a UCC form, check with the Secretary of State to be sure.

Source: Secretary of State's Office and Division of Revenue

District of Columbia

Corporations Division
Dept of Consumer and Regulatory Affairs
614 H Street, NW
Washington, DC 20001
(202) 727-7278

Dept of Finance and Revenue
300 Indiana Av, NW
Rm 4136
Washington, DC 20001
(202) 727-6020

Start-Up Requirements

Business Registration Requirements

Incorporation:
- File an Application for Reservation of Corporate Name. Cost: $25.00
- File two originally signed Articles of Incorporation in accordance with the D.C. Code with the Corporations Division. Cost: $120.00 is the minimum fee. It may be higher if you have more have more than $100,000 worth of authorized stock.

Limited Liability Company:
- File an Application to Reserve Name for Use by a Limited Liability Company. Cost: $25.00
- File the Articles of Organization pursuant to D.C. code. Cost: $100.00

Limited Liability Partnership:
- File the Application of Limited Liability Partnership. Cost: $50.00

Limited Partnership:
- File a Certificate of Limited Partnership. Cost: $70.00

Sole Proprietor and General Partnership:
- The requirement is that you contact the Department of Finance and Revenue to register. (See above address or call 727-6130.)

Foreign Entities:
- Corporations, limited liability companies, limited partnerships, and other businesses must file forms to transact business in the state. The fees and forms vary. They can be obtained from the Corporation's Division's address above.

Tax Registration Requirements

Sales and Withholding Tax: (1994 Information)
- To get a sales tax number, fill out FR-500 Combined Registration Application. This also registers you for other taxes. Cost: None listed. You might want to call the Department of Finance and Revenue for more information.

In-District Help and Information
- The Business Information Center (BIC) is in Washington, Phone: (202) 606-4000, ext. 266.
- The SBA Field Office is in: Washington, Phone: (202) 606-4000.
- Small Business Development Center, Howard University. Phone: (202) 806-1550.
- Call 1-800-8-ASK-SBA for SCORE locations.
- Securities Information: Securities Commission. Phone: (202) 626-5105.
- Web site: *www.ci.washington.dc.us*

Notes: Limited Partnerships must reaffirm their existence every three years. The Web site has all the business registration forms for downloading or printing.

Source: Corporation's Division of the Department of Consumer and Regulatory Affairs and Department of Finance and Revenue

Florida

Department of State
Division of Corporations

Department of Revenue
5050 W. Tennessee Street

PO Box 6327
Tallahassee, FL 32314
(904) 487-6052

Tallahassee, FL 32399-0100
(904) 488-9750

Start-Up Requirements

Business Registration Requirements

Incorporation:
- Reserve a name for 120 days. Cost: $35.00
- File one original and one copy of your Articles of Incorporation along with a letter of transmittal. Cost: $35.00 (A certified copy will also cost an additional $52.50)
- File a Certificate of Designation of Registered Agent/Registered Office. Cost: $35.00

Limited Liability Company:
- Reserve a name for 120 days. Cost: $35.00
- File the Articles of Organization. An Affidavit of Membership and Contributions must also accompany the Articles. Cost: $250.00. (A certified copy will also cost an additional $52.50)
- File a Certificate of Designation of Registered Agent/Registered Office. Cost: $35.00
- File a Certificate of Status. Cost: $8.75

Limited Liability Partnership:
- Reserve a name for 120 days. Cost: $35.00
- File a Statement of Registration of Registered Limited Liability Partnership. Cost: $100.00 per partner, $10,000 maximum.

Limited Partnership:
- Reserve a name for 120 days. Cost: $35.00
- Florida law has changed for partnerships. You now may be required to file a Partnership Registration Statement—Cost: $50.00—and a Statement of Partnership Authority—Cost: $25.00.
- File a Certificate of Limited Partnership along with an Affidavit of Capitol Contributions. Cost: $52.50 minimum and $1750.00 maximum based on the contribution of the limited partners.
- File a Certificate of Designation of Registered Agent/Registered Office. Cost: $35.00

General Partnership:
- Florida law has changed for partnerships. You now may be required to file a Partnership Registration Statement—Cost: $50.00—and a Statement of Partnership Authority—Cost: $25.00. Also, check with your local and county governments regarding their requirements.

Sole Proprietor:
- Check with your local and county governments.

Foreign Entities:
- Corporations, limited liability companies, limited partnerships, and other businesses must file forms to transact business in the state. The fees and forms vary. They can be obtained from the Department of State's address above.

Tax Registration Requirements

Sales Tax:
- To obtain a sales or use tax number, fill out form DR-1, Application to Collect Tax in Florida. Cost: $5.00
- Florida has no income tax so there is no withholding.

In-State Help and Information

- The Business Information Center (BIC) was not listed. Call (202) 205-6665 to see if Florida has set one up yet.
- The SBA Field Offices are in Coral Gables, Phone: (305) 536-5521 and Jacksonville, Phone: (904) 443-1900.
- Small Business Development Center, University of West Florida, Pensacola. Phone: (904) 444-2060.
- Call 1-800-8-ASK-SBA for SCORE locations.
- Minority Business Development Agency, Miami. Phone: (305) 536-5054.
- Securities Information: Bureau of Registrations, Division of Securities. Phone: (904) 488-9805.
- State Web site: *www.state.fl.us*

Notes: Florida's Department of Revenue sent a great deal of information, so be sure to write it. You may have to register a business name as a fictitious name. Write for details.

Source: Director of Cabinet Affairs and Department of Revenue

Georgia

Secretary of State
Corporations Division
Suite 315, West Tower
2 Martin Luther King Jr., Dr.
Atlanta, GA 30334-1530
(404) 657-1375

Department of Revenue
Centralized Taxpayer
Registration Unit
PO Box 74000
Atlanta, GA 30374
(404) 651-8651

Start-Up Requirements

Business Registration Requirements

Incorporation:

- Reserve a name by Business Services and Registration at (404) 656-2817. Your proposed name will be forwarded for final approval. Once your name has been confirmed, it is valid for a non-renewable 90-day period. Cost: None
- File the Articles of Incorporation. You write these yourself or with a lawyer pursuant to OCGA ss 14-2-202. 60.00
- Along with this, submit a Transmittal Information Form BR227.
- Also, you must publish a Notice of Intent to Incorporate in a newspaper in your registered agent's county (which will cost $40.00). Contact the Clerk of Superior Court in your county for more information.
- File a Name Registration. Cost: $20.00

Limited Liability Company:

- Reserve a name as above.
- File a Name Registration. Cost: $20.00
- File the Articles of Organization. Cost: $75.00
- Along with this, submit a Transmittal Information Form BR231.
- File a Name Registration. Cost: $20.00

Limited Liability Partnership:

- No information supplied.

Limited Partnership:

- Reserve a name as above.
- File a Certificate of Limited Partnership. Cost: $60.00
- Along with this, submit a Transmittal Information Form BR 246.
- File a Name Registration. Cost: $20.00

Sole Proprietor and General Partnership:

- Nothing needs to be done at the state level, check with the County Recorder or local offices.

Foreign Entities:

- Corporations, limited liability companies, limited partnerships, and other businesses must file forms to transact business in the state. The fees and forms vary. They can be obtained from the Secretary of State's address above.

Tax Registration Requirements

Sales and Withholding Tax:

- File the State Tax Registration Application, form CRF-002. Cost: None listed. This will register you for your sales and withholding tax. Other taxes are registered with different forms. The state will send information on these.

In-State Help and Information

- The Business Information Center (BIC) is in Atlanta, Phone: (404) 347-4749.
- The SBA Field Office is in Atlanta, Phone: (404) 347-4999.
- Small Business Development Center is at the University of Georgia, Athens, Phone: (706) 542-7662.
- The One Stop Capital Shop is in Atlanta, Phone: (404) 253-7675.
- Securities Information: Business Service and Regulations, Phone: (404) 656-2894.
- Minority Business Development Agency, Atlanta. Phone: (404) 730-3300.
- Call 1-800-ASK-SBA for SCORE locations.
- State Web site: *www.state.ga.us*

Notes: Georgia's agencies sent two complete information packages. The Department of Revenue holds sales and use tax workshops throughout the state. Call the state for more information. The transmittal forms are mailed to you after you submit a name reservation. Although we received good information, the requirements for Georgia are complicated. You might want to seek legal counsel.

Source: Secretary of State's Office and Department of Revenue

Hawaii

Dept of Commerce and Consumer Affairs
Business Registration Division
Post Office Box 40
Honolulu, HI 96810
(808) 586-2727

Dept of Taxation
PO Box 259
Honolulu, HI 96809
(808) 587-4242

Start-Up Requirements

Business Registration Requirements

Incorporation:

- Reserve a Corporate Name. Cost: $20.00

- File the Articles of Incorporation. Cost: $100.00
- Reserve Trade Name. Cost: $50.00

Limited Liability Company and Limited Liability Partnership:
- No information supplied.

Limited Partnership:
- Reserve your partnership name. Cost: $20.00
- File a Certificate of Limited Partnership. Cost: $25.00

General Partnership:
- Reserve your partnership name. Cost: $20.00
- File a Partnership Registration Statement. No application was included, so write for information. Cost: $25.00

Sole Proprietor:
- File an application in duplicate. No application was included, so write for information. Cost: $25.00 and a renewal fee.

Foreign Entities:
- Corporations, limited liability companies, limited partnerships, and other businesses must file forms to transact business in the state. The fees and forms vary. They can be obtained from the Department of Commerce and Consumer Affairs' address above.

Tax Registration Requirements

General Excise and Withholding Tax:
- File Form GEW-TA-RV-3 registers you for a variety of taxes. Cost: $20.00. Hawaii does not have a sales tax. It does have a general excise tax, which is levied against the business. The rate is 4% on the retail sales and 1/2 of 1% on wholesaling.

In-State Help and Information
- The Business Information Center (BIC) is in Honolulu and the phone number is (808) 522-8131.
- The SBA Field Office is in Honolulu, Phone: (808) 541-2990.
- Small Business Development Center is at the University of Hawaii, Hilo. Phone: (808) 933-3515.
- Call 1-800-ASK-SBA for SCORE locations.
- Securities Information: Business Registration Division, Phone: (808) 586-2744
- State Web site: *www.state.hi.us*

Notes: Please note that the general excise tax is different from sales tax in that it is imposed on the person doing business, not the consumer. We suggest you call for guidelines or visit the Web site first. Write for information on foreign entities.

Source: Department of Commerce and Consumer Affairs (Business Registration Division) and Department of Taxation

Idaho

Secretary of State
PO Box 83720
Boise, ID 83720-0080
(208) 334-2300

State Tax Commission
800 Park, Plaza IV
Boise, ID 83722
(208) 334-7660
1-800-92-7660

Start-Up Requirements

Business Registration Requirements

Incorporation:
- Submit an Application for Reservation of Corporate Name. Cost: $20.00
- Submit the Articles of Incorporation to the Secretary of State. Cost: $100.00 if completely typed, $120.00 if not typed.

Limited Liability Company:
- File a Name Reservation. Cost: $20.00
- File duplicates of the Articles of Organization with the Secretary of State. Cost: $100.00

Limited Liability Partnerships:
- File a Name Reservation. Cost: $20.00
- File the Registration of Limited Liability Partnership. Cost: $100.00

Limited Partnership:
- File a Name Reservation. Cost: $20.00 (If necessary)
- File duplicate originals of the Certificate of Limited Partnership. Cost: $100.00 if typed and with no attachments. $120.00 otherwise.

Sole Proprietor and General Partnership:
- Nothing needs to be done at the state level, but you might want to check county or local requirements.
- If needed, file the Certificate of Assumed Business Name. Cost: $20.00

Foreign Entities:
- Corporations, limited liability companies, limited partnerships, and other businesses must file forms to transact business in Indiana. The fees and forms vary. They can be obtained from the Secretary of State's address above.

Tax Registration Requirements

Sales and Withholding Tax:
- File form IBR-1, Idaho Business Registration Form, which will register you for sales, use, and withholding (among others) taxes. Cost: None.

In-State Help and Information
- The Business Information Center (BIC) is in Boise, the phone number is (208) 334-9077.
- The SBA Field Office is in Boise, Phone: (208) 334-1696.
- Small Business Development Center is at Boise State University, Phone (208) 385-1640.
- Call 1-800-ASK-SBA for SCORE locations.
- Securities Information: Idaho Department of Finance, Phone: (208) 334-3684.
- State Web site: *www.idoc.state.id.us*

Notes: Write to the Department of Commerce for the booklet Starting a Business in Idaho, an excellent guide with everything you will need to know. The address is Idaho Department of Commerce, 700 West State Street, PO Box 83720, Boise ID 83720. If a new company publicly issues stock, it must notify the Idaho Department of Finance in addition to the Securities and Exchange Commission.

Source: Secretary of State's Office and State Tax Commission.

State Requirements

Illinois

Secretary of State
Howlett Building
Springfield, IL 62756
(217) 782-6961

Dept of Revenue
101 W. Jefferson St
Springfield, IL 62794
(217) 782-3336

Start-Up Requirements

Business Registration Requirements

Incorporation:
- File a Reservation of Name. Cost: $25.00
- File BCA-2.10 Articles of Incorporation need to be filed in duplicate to the Secretary of State. Cost: $75.00 filing fee, plus a minimum franchise fee of $25.00 or 15/100 of 1% of the paid-in capital, whichever is higher.

Limited Liability Company:
- File the Application for Reservation of Name, form LLC-1.15. Cost: $300.00
- File Articles of Organization, form LLC-5.5. Cost: $500.00
- File the Application for Registration of Name, form LLC-45.20. Cost: $300.00

Limited Liability Partnership:
- File for a Limited Liability Partnership. Cost: $100.00 per partner.

Limited Partnership:
- File a Registration of Registered Agent, form LP-103c. Cost: $5.00
- File the Certificate of Limited Partnership, form LP-201. Cost: $75.00
- You may have other state requirements. Call for verification.

Sole Proprietor and General Partnership:
- Nothing needs to be done at the state level check your county and city officials.

Foreign Entities:
- Corporations, limited liability companies, limited partnerships, and other businesses must file forms to transact business in the state. The fees and forms vary. They can be obtained from the Secretary of State's address above.

Tax Registration Requirements

Sales and Withholding Tax:
- File the NUC-1 Tax Application form. This will register you for sales, income, and withholding taxes, among others. There may also be additional local taxes. Cost: None

In-State Help and Information
- The Business Information Center (BIC) is in Chicago, Phone: (312) 353-1825.
- The SBA Field Offices are in Chicago, Phone: (312) 353-5000 and Springfield, Phone: (217) 492-4416.
- Small Business Development Center is at the Department of Commerce and Community Affairs, Springfield. Phone (207) 524-5.
- Call 1-800-ASK-SBA for SCORE locations.
- Minority Business Development Agency, Chicago. Phone: (312) 353-0182.
- Securities Information: Securities Department, Phone: (217) 782-2256.
- State Web site: *www.sos.state.il.us*

Notes: Your check to the Secretary of State must be a certified check, cashier's check, Illinois attorney's or CPA check, or money order. Illinois operates under the Business Corporation Act. Some counties also have other taxes for mass transit, water, and home rule taxes. The Department of Revenue will send you a complete information kit if you ask for it. This contains forms and booklets.

Source: Secretary of State's Office and Department of Revenue

Indiana

Secretary of State
State Capitol
Indianapolis, IN 46204
(317) 232-6531

Dept of Revenue
Indiana Government Center North
Room N105
Indianapolis, IN 46204
(317) 233-4016

Start-Up Requirements

Business Registration Requirements

Incorporation:
- File an Application for Reserved Name with the Secretary of State. Cost: $20.00
- File Articles of Incorporation (State Form 4159) with the Secretary of State. Cost: $90.00

Limited Liability Company:
- File an Application for Reserved Name with the Secretary of State. Cost: $20.00
- File Articles of Organization. There is no preprinted form, the state will send a list of what must be in the articles. Cost: $90.00

Limited Liability Partnership:
- File an Application for Reserved Name with the Secretary of State. Cost: $20.00
- Submit a Limited Liability Partnership Registration. There is no preprinted form, the state will send a list of what must be in the registration. Cost: $90.00

Limited Partnership:
- Reserve a name by filing an Application for Reserved Name. Cost: $20.00
- Submit a Certificate of Limited Partnership to the Secretary of State. Include name of limited partnership, address of agent, general partners, dissolve date, and any other matters. Cost: $90.00

General Partnership and Sole Proprietor:
- Nothing needs to be done at the state level. File at the County Recorder.

Foreign Entities:
- Corporations, limited liability companies, limited partnerships, and other businesses must file forms to transact business in the state. The fees and forms vary. They can be obtained from the Secretary of State's address above.

Tax Registration Requirements

Sales and Withholding Tax:
- All taxes including sales, withholding, corporate, use, and excise taxes are registered on form BT-1, Indiana Department of Revenue Business Tax Application. Cost: $25.00.

In-State Help and Information
- The Business Information Center (BIC) phone number was not listed. Call (202) 205-6665 to see if Indiana has set one up yet.
- The SBA Field Office is in Indianapolis, Phone: (317) 226-7272.
- Small Business Development Center is at the Economic Development Council in Indianapolis. Phone: (317) 264-6871
- Call 1-800-ASK-SBA for SCORE locations.
- Securities Information: Securities Division, Phone: (317) 232-6681.
- State Web site: *www.state.in.us*

Notes: Write and ask for the publications Starting a Business in Indiana, Indiana Corporation Guide, and/or Indiana Limited Partnership Guide. Annual reports are due and have a $15.00 fee. Write the State Department of Revenue for the lfollowing brochures: General Requirements for Indiana Businesses, Indiana Retail Stales Tax and Use Guide, and Withholding Instructions for Indiana State and County Income Taxes.

Source: Secretary of State's Office and Department of Revenue

Iowa

Secretary of State
Corporations Division
Hoover Building
Des Moines, IA 50319
(515) 281-5204

Dept of Revenue and Finance
Hoover State Office Bldg
Des Moines, IA 50319
(515) 281-3204

Start-Up Requirements

Business Registration Requirements

Incorporation: (1994 information)
- Reserve a corporate name with the Application to Reserve Corporate Name. Send it to the Secretary of State. Cost: $10.00
- File an Articles of Incorporation including the usual addresses, names, shares, provisions, and bylaws. Cost: $50.00

Limited Liability Company:
- Contact the Iowa Secretary of State at the address above for information.

Limited Liability Partnership:
- File an Application for LLP. Cost: None listed. Call the state.

Limited Partnership: (1994 information)
- File an Application to Reserve Name. Cost: $10.00
- File an Application for Certificate of Registration of Limited Partnership with the Secretary of State. Cost: $100.00

Sole Proprietor and General Partnership: (1994 information)
- Nothing needs to be done at the state level. See the County Recorder or your city officials for licensing information.

Foreign Entities:
- Corporations, limited liability companies, limited partnerships, and other businesses must file forms to transact business in the state. The fees and forms vary. They can be obtained from the Secretary of State's address above.

Tax Registration Requirements

Sales and Withholding Tax:

- Obtain a Retail Sales Tax permit number and/or a Use Tax number and withholding by filing Iowa Business Tax Registration. Cost: None listed. Iowa has a 5% sales tax. You will need Sales Tax Exemption certificates for exempt sales.

In-State Help and Information

- The Business Information Center (BIC) phone number was not listed. Call (202) 205-6665 to see if Iowa has set one up yet.
- The SBA Field Offices are in Cedar Rapids, Phone: (319) 362-6405; and Des Moines, Phone: (515) 284-4422.
- Small Business Development Center is at Iowa State University, Ames. Phone: (515) 292-6351.
- Bureau of Small Business Development, 200 East Grand, Des Moines IA 50309, Phone: (515) 242-4750 or 1-800-532-1216
- Call 1-800-ASK-SBA for SCORE locations.
- Securities Information: Securities Bureau Enforcement, Phone: (515) 281-4441.
- State Web site: *www.state.ia.us*

Notes: We received poor information in reply to our request to the Secretary of State. We suggest you call the Secretary of State, or better yet, call the Bureau of Small Business Development for information. Write the state Department of Revenue and Finance for excellent information on sales and other taxes.

Source: Secretary of State's Office and Department of Revenue and Finance

Kansas

Secretary of State
2nd Floor, State House
Topeka, KS 66612-1594
(913) 296-4564

Department of Revenue
Docking State Office Bldg.
Topeka, KS 66612-1588
(913) 296-0222

Start-Up Requirements

Business Registration Requirements

Incorporation:

- File a Reservation of Name form. Cost: $20.00
- Fill out form CF, for Profit Articles of Incorporation. This must be submitted in duplicate to the Secretary of State. Cost: $75.00

Limited Liability Company:

- File a Reservation of Name form. Cost: $20.00
- File for a Limited Liability Company. Cost: $150.00

Limited Liability Partnership:

- File a Reservation of Name form. Cost: $20.00
- File a Limited Liability Partnership Registration. Cost: $75.00 per partner.

Limited Partnership:

- Create and file a Certificate of Limited Partnership including name of partnership, address of registered office and agent, name and business or residence of each general partner, date upon which it dissolves, and any other matters you deem necessary. Send to the Secretary of State. Cost: $150.00

Sole Proprietor and General Partnership:
- Contact your County Recorder or Clerk and your local government for licensing or permits.

Foreign Entities:
- Corporations, limited liability companies, limited partnerships, and other businesses must file forms to transact business in the state. The fees and forms vary. They can be obtained from the Secretary of State's address above.

Tax Registration Requirements

Sales and Withholding Tax:
- File form BT/rg-16, Business Tax Application. This will register you for a variety of taxes including sales and withholding. Cost: None

In-State Help and Information
- The Business Information Center (BIC) phone number was not listed. Call (202) 205-6665 to see if Kansas has set one up yet.
- The SBA Field Office is in Wichita, Phone: (316) 269-6616.
- Small Business Development Center is at Wichita State University, Wichita. Phone: (316) 689-3193.
- One Stop Capital Shop, Kansas City KS, Phone: (913) 371-6007.
- Call 1-800-ASK-SBA for SCORE locations.
- First Stop Clearing House, Topeka. Phone: (913) 296-5298.
- Securities Information: Office of Securities Commissioner, Phone: (913) 296-3307.
- Web site: *www.ink.org/public/sos* or *www.state.ks.us*

Notes: A call to the First Stop Clearinghouse would not be a wasted effort—the state suggests you do this. You can request information on all aspects of starting a business in Kansas from this location. Ask for the Steps to Success: A Guide to Starting a Business in Kansas. You may need to file a UCC financing statement. Call the state.

Source: Secretary of State's Office and Department of Revenue

Kentucky

Secretary of State
State Capitol Bldg
Frankfort, KY 40601
(502) 564-2848

Revenue Cabinet
200 Fair Oaks Lane
Frankfort, KY 40620
(502) 564-3226

Start-Up Requirements

Business Registration Requirements

Incorporation:
- File the Application of Reservation of Name form. Cost: $15.00
- File Articles of Incorporation according to the specific needs of each corporation. You must state name, number of shares, address of registered office and agent, mailing address of principal office, and name and mailing address of each incorporator. Cost: $50.00 is the minimum fee—check with the Web site for more on fees.

Limited Liability Company:
- File the Application of Reservation of Name form. Cost: $15.00

- File the Articles of Organization. Cost: $40.00

Limited Liability Partnership:
- File the Application of Reservation of Name form. Cost: $15.00
- File the Statement of Registration. Cost: $200.00

Limited Partnership:
- File the Application of Reservation of Name form. Cost: $15.00
- File a Certificate of Limited Partnership. Cost: $40.00

General Partnership:
- If you are using an assumed name, file with the County Clerk and the Secretary of State.

Sole Proprietor:
- Filed strictly in the County Clerk's office and only if you are using an assumed name.

Foreign Entities:
- Corporations, limited liability companies, limited partnerships, and other businesses must file forms to transact business in the state. The fees and forms vary. They can be obtained from the Secretary of State's address above.

Tax Registration Requirements

Sales and Withholding Tax:
- File a Kentucky Tax Registration Application, form 10A100. Cost: $10.00 for each business location.

In-State Help and Information

- The Business Information Center (BIC) phone number was not listed. Call (202) 205-6665 to see if Kentucky has set one up yet.
- The SBA Field Office is in Louisville, Phone: (502) 582-5971.
- Small Business Development Center is the University of Kentucky, Lexington. Phone: (606) 257-7668.
- One Stop Capital Shop, Somerset. Phone: (606) 677-6080.
- Call 1-800-ASK-SBA for SCORE locations.
- Business Information Clearinghouse, Phone: 1-800-626-2250.
- Taxpayer Ombudsman, Phone: (502) 564-7822.
- Securities Information: Department of Financial Institutions, Phone: (502) 573-3390.
- State Web site: *www.state.ky.us*

Notes: Copies of the *Kentucky Corporation Law and Rules* are available for $8.00 each by writing to the Secretary of State, Corporate Division. Ask for the *Kentucky Enterprise* publication from the Revenue Cabinet for information on starting a small business.

Source: Secretary of State's Office and Revenue Cabinet

Louisiana

Secretary of State
Commercial Division
PO Box 94125
Baton Rouge, LA 70804-9125
(504) 925-4704

Dept of Revenue and Taxation
330 N Ardenwood
Baton Rouge, LA 70804
(504) 925-7680

Start-Up Requirements

Business Registration Requirements

Incorporation:
- Reserve a name from the Secretary of State by using form #398, Reservation of a Corporate Name. Cost: $20.00
- File the Articles of Incorporation, form #399, with the Secretary of State. $60.00
- File the Domestic Corporation Initial Report along with the Articles of Incorporation, form #341. Cost: None

Limited Liability Company:
- Reserve a name from the Secretary of State by using form #974, Reservation of a Limited Liability Company Name. Cost: $20.00
- File the Articles of Organization. No form is provided, but you will have a guideline to write it. Cost: $60.00
- File the Limited Liability Company Initial Report. Cost: None

Limited Liability Partnership:
- File an Application Registration of Limited Liability Partnership, form #975. Cost: $100.00

Limited Partnership:
- Fill out form #342 and submit the original. Also, submit a multiple original of the partnership contract signed by all partners or a notarized certified copy. Also file for registry with the recorder of mortgages in your parish of principal place of business. Cost: $75.00

General Partnership:
- The state made no distinction between limited and general partnerships, so check first with the state or your lawyer. As always check local and parish government.

Sole Proprietor:
- Filed with Clerk of Court in Parish of domicile.

Foreign Entities:
- Corporations, limited liability companies, limited partnerships, and other businesses must file forms to transact business in the state. The fees and forms vary. They can be obtained from the Secretary of State's address above.

Tax Registration Requirements

Sales Tax: (1994 Information)
- File a Central Registration Application. Cost: None

Withholding Tax:
- Contact the Louisiana Department of Revenue and Taxation for information.

In-State Help and Information
- The Business Information Center (BIC) phone number was not listed. Call (202) 205-6665 to see if Louisiana has set one up yet.
- The SBA Field Office is in New Orleans, Phone: (504) 589-6685.
- Small Business Development Center is at Northeast Louisiana University, Monroe. Phone: (318) 342-5506.
- Call 1-800-ASK-SBA for SCORE locations.
- Securities Information: Office of Financial Institutions, Commissioner of Securities, Phone: (504) 568-5515.

- First Stop Shop, Phone: 1-800-259-0001.
- State Web site: *www.state.la.us*

Notes: Within thirty days after filing to become a corporation, a multiple original of the Articles and the Initial report (or a copy of each certified by the Secretary of State) and a copy of the Certificate of Incorporation must be filed with the Parish Recorder in your company's parish. "Doing Business in Louisiana" is a book of forms, costs $4.00, and is available from the Secretary of State's Office.

Source: Secretary of State's Office and Department of Revenue and Taxation

Maine

Secretary of State
Division of Corporations
State House Station #101
Augusta, ME 04333
(207) 287-4195

Bureau of Taxation
PO Box 1065
State Office Bldg
Augusta, ME 04332-1065
(207) 287-2336

Start-Up Requirements

Business Registration Requirements

Incorporation:
- File an Application for Reservation of Name. Cost: $20.00
- File the Maine Articles of Incorporation (Form No. MBCA-6Rev.96) with the Secretary of State. Cost: The minimum fee is $105.00. However, it could be more based on how much capital stock is authorized.
- You may need to register your trade name for all types of business entity.

Limited Liability Company and
Limited Liability Partnership:
- File an Application for Reservation of Name. Cost: $20.00
- File the Articles of Organization. Cost: $250.00

Limited Liability Partnership:
- File an Application for Reservation of Name. Cost: $20.00
- File a Certificate of Limited Liability Partnership. Cost: $250.00

Limited Partnership:
- File an Application for Reservation of Name. Cost: $20.00
- File a Certificate of Limited Partnership with the Secretary of State. Cost: $250.00

Sole Proprietor and General Partnership:
- Nothing needs to be done at the state level, check with your Municipal Clerk or county officials to file your business.

Foreign Entities:
- Corporations, limited liability companies, limited partnerships, and other businesses must file forms to transact business in the state. The fees and forms vary. They can be obtained from the Secretary of State's address above.

Tax Registration Requirements

Sales and Withholding Tax:
- File an Application for Tax Registration, which will also register you for other taxes. Cost: None

In-State Help and Information
- The Business Information Center (BIC) is in Lewiston, Phone: (207) 782-5355.
- The SBA Field Office is in Augusta, Phone: (207) 622-8378.
- Small Business Development Center is at the University of Southern Maine, Portland. Phone: (207) 780-4420.
- One Stop Business Licensing Center, Phone: 1-800-872-3838.
- Call 1-800-ASK-SBA for SCORE locations.
- Securities Information: Bureau of Banking Securities Division, Phone: (207) 624-8551.
- State Web site: *www.state.me.us*

Notes: If someone executes the articles on behalf of your corporation, a certification that the person was authorized to do so must be submitted too by an officer of the corporation. The state sent only forms, no booklets or other materials. We suggest you write the state for additional information.

Source: Secretary of State's Office and Bureau of Taxation

Maryland

Secretary of State
State House
Annapolis, MD 21401
(301) 974-3421

Comptroller of Treasury
Central Registration Unit
301 West Preston St
Baltimore, MD 21201-2383
(301) 225-1313

Start-Up Requirements

Business Registration Requirements

Incorporation:
- For a stock company, reserve a corporate name with the state. This will reserve the name for thirty days. Cost: $7.00
- Next, file the Articles of Incorporation for a Stock Company. Maryland provides a one page form if you wish. You file with the Department of Assessments and Taxation. You may want to create your own, however. Cost: $40.00 minimum. More if you have more than $100,000 worth of stock.

Limited Liability Company and Limited Liability Partnership:
- No information supplied.

Limited Partnership:
- Reserve a limited partnership name. The name is held for thirty days. Cost: $7.00
- File a Certificate of Limited Partnership with the state. Cost: $50.00

Sole Proprietor and General Partnership:
- Nothing needs to be done at the state level, check your local or county government.

Foreign Entities:
- Corporations, limited liability companies, limited partnerships, and other businesses must file forms to transact business in the state. The fees and forms vary. They can be obtained from the Secretary of State's address above.

Tax Registration Requirements

Sales and Withholding Tax:
- File a Combined Registration Application, which registers you for a variety of taxes. Cost: None

In-State Help and Information
- The Business Information Center (BIC) is in Baltimore, Phone: (410) 605-0990.
- The SBA Field Office is in Baltimore, Phone: (410) 962-4392.
- Small Business Development Center is at the University of Maryland, College Park, Phone: (301) 405-2147.
- Call 1-800-ASK-SBA for SCORE locations.
- One Stop Capital Shop, Baltimore. Phone (410) 783-4222.
- Securities Information: Division of Securities, Phone: (410) 576-6360.
- State Web site: *www.state.md.us*

Notes: Write the state for more information. Annual reports are due by April 15 of each year. Note, do not start business unless a written notice of acceptance of the Articles of Incorporation is received. Write for guides and pamphlets on incorporating and forming limited partnerships.

Source: Secretary of State's Office and Comptroller of the Treasury

Massachusetts

Secretary of the Commonwealth
Corporations Division
One Ashburton Place,
Boston, MA 02108
(617) 727-9640

Dept of Revenue
PO Box 7011
17th Floor Boston, MA 02204
(617) 887-6367

Start-Up Requirements

Business Registration Requirements

Incorporation:
- Reserve a name for thirty days with the Corporations Division of the Secretary of the Commonwealth. Cost: $15.00
- File Articles of Organization, a two-page, four-sided form. Cost: 1/10 of 1% of the capital stock, with a minimum fee of $200.00.

Limited Liability Company:
- You may want to reserve a name. The state was unclear on this.
- File the Certificate of Organization with the Secretary of the Commonwealth. Cost: $500.00

Limited Liability Partnership:
- You may want to reserve a name. The state was unclear on this.
- File for registration with the Secretary of the Commonwealth. Cost: $500.00

Limited Partnership:
- Reserve a name for thirty days as above. Cost: $15.00
- File a Certificate of Limited Partnership with the Secretary of the Commonwealth. The guidelines are provided if you write for them. Cost: $200.00

State Requirements

General Partnership:
- File a DBA (Doing Business As) at the local city or town hall.

Sole Proprietor:
- If it is under your name, you have no state requirements. If you are doing business with a name other than your own, file a DBA with the local city or town hall.

Foreign Entities:
- Corporations, limited liability companies, limited partnerships, and other businesses must file forms to transact business in the state. The fees and forms vary. They can be obtained from the Secretary of the Commonwealth's address above.

Tax Registration Requirements

Sales and Withholding Tax:
- File form TA-1, Application for Original Registration, which is used for most tax registration. Cost: $10.00
- Schedule TA-3 may be required as well. Call the state to find out.

In-State Help and Information
- The Business Information Center (BIC) is in Boston, Phone: (617) 565-5615.
- The SBA Field Office is in Boston, Phone: (617) 565-8415.
- Small Business Development Center is at the University of Massachusetts, Amherst, Phone: (413) 545-6301.
- Call 1-800-ASK-SBA for SCORE locations.
- One Stop Capital Shop, Boston. Phone (617) 445-3413.
- Securities Information: Office of Secretary of State, Securities Division, Phone: (617) 727-3548.
- Minority Business Development Agency is in Boston. Phone: (617) 565-6850.
- State Web site: *www.state.ma.us*

Notes: Professional corporations must file Articles of Organization for a $200.00 fee. Annual reports for corporations are due 2 1/2 months after the corporation's fiscal year end and cost $85.00. Ask specifically for the publication "Organizing a Business Corporation", as well as "Starting a New Business in Massachusetts", which the Department of Revenue sent us. Do not forget local license and permit requirements.

Source: Secretary of the Commonwealth's Office and Department of Revenue

Michigan

Dept of Consumer Services
PO Box 30222
Lansing, MI 48909
(517) 334-6327

Bureau of Revenue
Dept of Treasury
Lansing, MI 48922
(517) 373-0888

Start-Up Requirements

Business Registration Requirements

Incorporation:
- File an Application for Reservation of Name. Cost: $10.00
- File the Articles of Incorporation with the Department of Consumer Services. Cost: Minimum fees would be $60.00. It could be more depending on how many shares of stock you have.

Limited Liability Company:
- File a Reservation of Name form. Cost: $10.00
- File the Articles of Organization. Cost: $50.00

Limited Liability Partnership:
- File for a CoPartnership by filling out a Certificate of CoPartnership with the County Clerk.
- Then file an Application to Register a Limited Liability Partnership. Cost: None given.

Limited Partnership:
- File the Application for Reservation of Name. Cost: $10.00
- File the Certificate of Limited Partnership. Cost: $10.00

and CoPartnership:
- File a Certificate of CoPartnership with the County Clerk. You may need to file an assumed name in each county you do business as well.

Sole Proprietor:
- File at the County Clerk for an assumed business name.

Foreign Entities:
- Corporations, limited liability companies, limited partnerships, and other businesses must file forms to transact business in the state. The fees and forms vary. They can be obtained from the Department of Consumer Services' address above.

Tax Registration Requirements

Sales and Withholding Tax:
- File Michigan Department of Treasury and Mesa Registration for Michigan Taxes. This registers you for up to seven different taxes. Cost: $1.00, which is for a sales tax license and is renewed annually.

In-State Help and Information

- The Business Information Center (BIC) was not listed. Call (202) 205-6665 to see if Michigan has set one up yet.
- The SBA Field Offices are in Detroit, Phone: (313) 226-6075; and Marquette, Phone: (906) 225-1108.
- Small Business Development Center is at Wayne State University, Detroit, Phone: (313) 577-4848.
- Call 1-800-ASK-SBA for SCORE locations.
- One Stop Capital Shop, Detroit. Phone (313) 965-1100.
- Securities Information: Department of Commerce: Corporations and Securities Bureau, Phone: (517) 334-6200.
- State Web site: *www.cis.state.mi.us*

Notes: For more information, please contact the Michigan Department of Consumer and Industry Services. This department, rather than the Secretary of State, handles incorporations and limited partnerships.

Source: Michigan Department of Consumer and Industry Services, Corporations and Securities Bureau and Office, and The Department of Treasury

Minnesota

Secretary of State
Division of Corporations
180 State Office Building
100 Constitution Ave.
St. Paul, MN 55155
(612) 296-2803

Department of Revenue
Mail Station 4410
St. Paul, MN 55146-4410
(612) 282-5225 or
1-800-657-3605

Start-Up Requirements

Business Registration Requirements

Incorporation:
- There is one form to fill out. This is form SC-00171-02, Articles of Incorporation Chapter 302A. This is a one page, two-sided form. Return to the Secretary of State. Cost: $35.00 for a filing fee and $100.00 for an incorporation fee, for a total of $135.00.

Limited Liability Company and Limited Liability Partnership:
- Contact the Minnesota Secretary of State at the address above for information.

Limited Partnership: (1994 information)
- The form for a limited partnership is SC-00188-02, Certificate of Limited Partnership. It is one page, two-sided. Cost: $35.00 filing fee, plus a $60.00 initial fee for a total of $95.00.

Sole Proprietor and General Partnership: (1994 information)
- Nothing needs to be done at the state level unless you need to file a Certificate of Assumed Name. Otherwise, check your county and local officials for licensing and permits.

Foreign Entities:
- Corporations, limited liability companies, limited partnerships, and other businesses must file forms to transact business in the state. The fees and forms vary. They can be obtained from the Secretary of State's address above.

Tax Registration Requirements

Sales and Withholding Tax:
- File an Application for Business Registration, which registers you for a variety of taxes. Cost: None

In-State Help and Information
- The Business Information Center (BIC) was not listed. Call (202) 205-6665 to see if Minnesota has set one up yet.
- The SBA Field Office is in Minneapolis, Phone: (612) 370-2324.
- Small Business Development Center is at the Department of Trade and Economic Development, St. Paul, Phone: (612) 297-5770.
- Call 1-800-ASK-SBA for SCORE locations.
- Securities Information: Department of Commerce: Office of the Commission, Phone: (612) 296-4523.
- State Web site: *www.cis.state.mn.us*

Notes: The Articles of Incorporation form and the Certificate of Limited Partnership are merely guides. Should your business have requirements not covered on the forms, the state recommends you cover this by drafting your own Articles or Certificate. Call 1-800-657-3777 to request a free copy of the Minnesota sales and use tax instructions booklet. In addition, if you conduct business under a name other than your legal name, file a Certificate of Assumed Name ($25.00).

Source: Secretary of State's Office and Department of Revenue

Mississippi

Secretary of State
Business Services Division
PO Box 136
Jackson, MS 39205-0136
(601) 359-1633
(800) 256-3494

State Tax Commission
102 Woolfolk Bldg
Jackson, MS 39201
(601) 359-1100

Start-Up Requirements

Business Registration Requirements

Incorporation: : (1994 Information)
- Fill out the application to reserve a name. A copy is included in the Incorporating in Mississippi booklet. The name is reserved for 180 days. Cost: $25.00
- Next, fill out the Articles of Incorporation and return to the Secretary of State. This is a simple form, but you may use your own. In that case, it must be on 8 1/2" by 11" paper, and you must use just one side. Submit the original and one copy, and a stamped, self-addressed envelope. Cost: $50.00

Limited Liability Company and
Limited Liability Partnership:
- Contact the Mississippi Secretary of State for information.

Limited Partnership: (1994 Information)
- Fill out the application to reserve a name. Cost: $25.00
- Fill out the Certificate of Mississippi Limited Partnership in duplicate originals and send to the Secretary of State. If you use your own paper, type on only one side of the paper. Include a stamped, self-addressed envelope for return mailing of evidenced copy of filing. Cost: $50.00 (Note, a notary public must witness signatures and sign the document.)

Sole Proprietor and General Partnership: (1994 Information)
- Nothing needs to be done at the state level, check your county and local governments.

Foreign Entities:
- Corporations, limited liability companies, limited partnerships, and other businesses must file forms to transact business in the state. The fees and forms vary. They can be obtained from the Secretary of State's address above.

Tax Registration Requirements

Sales Tax: (1994 Information)
- File Form 60-007, Registration Application. Cost: None.

Withholding Tax:
- Contact the Mississippi State Tax Commission at the address above for information.

In-State Help and Information

- The Business Information Center (BIC) was not listed. Call (202) 205-6665 to see if Mississippi has set one up yet.
- The SBA Field Offices are in Gulfport, Phone: (601) 863-4449 and Jackson, Phone: (601) 965-4378.
- Small Business Development Center is at the University of Mississippi, University, Phone: (601) 232-5001.
- Call 1-800-ASK-SBA for SCORE locations.
- Securities Information: Secretary of State, Securities and Business Services, Phone: (601) 359-6364.
- State Web site: *www.cis.state.ms.us*

Notes: Ask for the publication Incorporating in Mississippi, from the Secretary of State. Articles of incorporation cannot be filed unless the corporation has paid all filing fees and franchise taxes imposed by law. Mississippi has no state property tax, low interest finance programs, and other incentives for businesses.

Source: Secretary of State's Office and State Tax Commission

Missouri

Secretary of State
PO Box 778
Jefferson City, MO 65102
(573) 751-2359
or (573) 751-4544

Dept of Revenue
1617 Southridge Drive
PO Box 385
Jefferson City, MO 65105
(573) 751-7191
1-800-877-6881(Forms only)

Start-Up Requirements

Business Registration Requirements

Incorporation:
- Pursue a name check by calling (573) 751-3317. If the name you want is available, file the forms for application or simply write a letter requesting the name to the Secretary of State. Cost: $25.00
- File the Articles of Incorporation with the Secretary of State. It must be notarized. Cost: Varies depending upon amount of authorized capital. For example, for $30,000 or less of capital, your fee would be $55.00; for each additional $10,000 of capital, it rises by $5.00. Then, add $3.00 for a filing fee to that total. Thus the minimum would be $58.00.

Limited Liability Company:
- Reserve a name as above. Cost: $25.00
- File the Articles of Organization with the Secretary of State. Cost: $105.00

Limited Liability Partnership:
- Reserve a name as above. Cost: $25.00
- File an Application for Registration of a Limited Liability Partnership with the Secretary of State. Cost: $105.00

Limited Partnership:
- Reserve a name as above. Cost: $25.00
- File a Certificate of Limited Partnership with the Secretary of State. Cost: $105.00

Sole Proprietor and General Partnership:

- Nothing at state level unless you use a fictitious name, which has a $7.00 fee. Check your county government.

Foreign Entities:

- Corporations, limited liability companies, limited partnerships, and other businesses must file forms to transact business in the state. The fees and forms vary. In Missouri, though, some foreign corporations are allowed to do certain activities without registration. Check with the Secretary of State's office.

Tax Registration Requirements

Sales and Withholding Tax:

- File one form, 2643, which will also register you for other taxes. There is no cost, but you may have to file a bond to cover the cost of estimated tax. Write for information. The tax is 4.225% (plus any applicable local sales tax).

In-State Help and Information

- The Business Information Centers (BICs) are in Kansas City, Phone: (816) 374-6675; and St. Louis, Phone: (314) 854-6861.
- The SBA Field Offices are in Kansas City, Phone: (816) 374-6380; Springfield, Phone: (417) 864-7670; and St. Louis, Phone: (314) 539-6600.
- Small Business Development Center is at the University of Missouri, Columbia. Phone: (314) 882-0344.
- Call 1-800-ASK-SBA for SCORE locations.
- The One Stop Capital Shop for Kansas and Missouri is in Kansas City, KS; Phone: (913) 371-6007.
- Securities Information: Securities Division, Phone: (573) 751-4136.
- State Web site: *www.state.mo.us*

Notes: Missouri suggest that you (or your lawyer) use Missouri forms as they comply completely with Missouri law. Note, Article Eight of the Articles of Incorporation must specifically state what you will do to make a profit.

Source: Secretary of State's Office and Department of Revenue

Montana

Secretary of State
PO Box 202801
Helena, MT 59620-2801
(406) 444-3665

Dept of Revenue
PO Box 5835
Helena, MT 59620-5835
(406) 444-3388

Start-Up Requirements

Business Registration Requirements

Incorporation:

- File an Application for Reservation of Name. Cost: $10.00
- File the Articles of Incorporation. Cost: $70.00 is the minimum fee. It could go higher depending on your shares.

Limited Liability Company:

- File an Application for Reservation of Name. Cost: $10.00

- File Your Articles of Organization. Cost: $70.00

Limited Liability Partnership:
- File an Application for Reservation of Name. Cost: $10.00
- File an Application for Registration with the Secretary of State. Cost: $70.00

Limited Partnership:
- File an Application for Reservation of Name. Cost: $10.00
- File for a Certificate of Limited Partnership (one original and a copy). Cost: $20.00

Sole Proprietor and General Partnership:
- File an Assumed Business Name with the Secretary of State. Cost: $20.00
- Otherwise see local authorities for licenses.

Foreign Entities:
- Corporations, limited liability companies, limited partnerships, and other businesses must file forms to transact business in the state. The fees and forms vary. They can be obtained from the Secretary of State's address above.

Tax Registration Requirements

Withholding Tax:
- Montana has no sales tax. Call for any other taxes.
- Withholding is registered for by calling the help number at (406) 444-3388. Unfortunately, the Revenue office did not send us any other pertinent information.

In-State Help and Information
- The Business Information Center (BIC) is in Helena, Phone: (406) 441-1081.
- The SBA Field Office is in Helena, Phone: (406) 441-1081.
- Small Business Development Center is at the Department of Commerce, Helena. Phone: (406) 444-4780.
- Call 1-800-ASK-SBA for SCORE locations.
- Securities Information: Securities Department, Phone: (406) 444-2040.
- State Web site: *www.state.mt.us*

Notes: Ask for the Secretary of State's Montana, We Mean Business booklet. It's great. Annual reports are due each year for corporations and cost either $10.00, $20.00, or $30.00, depending on when you file.

Source: Secretary of State's Office and Department of Revenue

Nebraska

Secretary of State
1301, State Capitol
PO Box 94608
Lincoln, NE 68509
(402) 471-4079

Dept of Revenue
PO Box 94818
Lincoln, NE 68509-4818
(402) 471-2971

Start-Up Requirements

Business Registration Requirements

Incorporation:
- Reserve a corporate name. Cost: $15.00
- File the Articles of Incorporation. Consult the statutes on what to include or contact an attorney. The fees range from $40.00 to over $200.00

- Register your trade name. Cost: $100.00

Limited Liability Companies and Limited Liability Partnerships:
- No information sent.

Limited Partnership:
- Reserve a corporate name. Cost: $15.00
- File a Nebraska limited partnership certificate with your name, agent and office, and general partners with address and signatures. Send it in duplicate. Cost: $200.00 plus $3.00 per page
- You may need to register your trade name. Call the Secretary of State.

Sole Proprietor and General Partnership:
- Consult your County Recorder or local officials. Nothing needs to be done at the state level. You may need to register your trade name. Call the Secretary of State.

Foreign Entities:
- Corporations, limited liability companies, limited partnerships, and other businesses must file forms to transact business in the state. The fees and forms vary. They can be obtained from the Secretary of State's address above.

Tax Registration Requirements

Sales and Withholding Tax:
- File Form 20, Nebraska Tax Application. This registers you for withholding, sales tax permits, and other miscellaneous taxes. Cost: $10.00

In-State Help and Information

- The Business Information Center (BIC) is in Omaha, Phone: (402) 221-3606.
- The SBA Field Office is in Omaha, Phone: (402) 221-4691.
- Small Business Development Center is at the University of Nebraska, Omaha. Phone: (402) 554-2521.
- Call 1-800-ASK-SBA for SCORE locations.
- Securities Information: Department of Banking and Finance, Phone: (402) 471-3445.
- State Web site: *www.state.nb.us*

Notes: If starting a limited liability company or partnership, call the state or talk to a lawyer.

Source: Secretary of State's Office and Department of Revenue

Nevada

Secretary of State
State Capitol Complex
Carson City, NV 89710
(702) 687-3471

Dept of Taxation
1340 S Curry St
 Carson City, NV 89710
(702) 885-4892

Start-Up Requirements

Business Registration Requirements

Incorporation:
- Reserve a corporate name from the Secretary of State. Cost: $20.00

- File Articles of Incorporation. There is no set form, but write and ask for the guidelines, which are quite good. Cost: $10 for each certified copy of the articles and resident agent's acceptance, *plus* a fee that varies with the amount of capital, starting at $125 for under $25,000 of stock.
- File an Annual list with the Secretary of State within sixty days. This is a list of officers and the registered agent. Cost: $85.00

Limited Liability Company:
- Reserve a name from the Secretary of State. Cost: $20.00
- File the Articles of Organization. Cost: $10.00 for each certified copy and $125.00 filing fee.

Limited Partnership:
- Reserve a name from the Secretary of State. Cost: $20.00
- File the Certificate of Limited Partnership, form LP-1. Cost: $125.00

Sole Proprietor and General Partnership:
- Check with the County Clerk.

Foreign Entities:
- Corporations, limited liability companies, limited partnerships, and other businesses must file forms to transact business in the state. The fees and forms vary. They can be obtained from the Secretary of State's address above.

Tax Registration Requirements

Sales Tax:
- To obtain a license, fill out the Combined Application for Seller's Permit and Registration (two parts). Cost: $3.00 for each location.

Withholding Tax:
- Nevada has no personal income tax.

In-State Help and Information
- The Business Information Center (BIC) phone number was not listed. Call (202) 205-6665 to see if Nevada has set one up yet.
- The SBA Field Office is in Las Vegas, Phone: (702) 388-6611.
- Small Business Development Center is at the University of Nevada, Reno. Phone: (702) 784-1717.
- Call 1-800-ASK-SBA for SCORE locations.
- Securities Information: Secretary of State Securities Division, Phone: (702) 486-2444.
- State Web site: *www.state.nv.us*

Notes: Write the state for a complete, up-to-date list of the requirements. You may have to file security equal to three times the monthly tax liability—the minimum is $100. Talk to your lawyer.

Source: Secretary of State's Office and Department of Taxation

New Hampshire

Secretary of State
Room 204 State House
Concord, NH 03301
(603) 271-3244

Dept of Revenue Admin
61 So. Spring St, PO Box 457
Concord, NH 03302-0457
(603) 271-2191

Start-Up Requirements

Business Registration Requirements

Incorporation:
- Reserve a Corporate Name with Form 1. Cost: $15.00
- Fill out a Securities Certification form 11-A certification stating the corporations capital stock has been registered. to incorporate. Mail to the Secretary of State's office. Cost: $50.00
- Mail Securities Certification form with Form No. 11, Articles of Incorporation, a two page document. Send to Secretary of State. Mail one original and one exact copy. Cost: $35.00

Limited Liability Company:
- Reserve a Name with Form 1. Cost: $15.00
- File Certificate of Formation LLC1. Cost: $35.00

Limited Partnership:
- File a Limited Partnership Reservation (name). Cost: $15.00
- File a Limited Partnership Application (LP-1) and a Securities Certification (LP-1A). Cost: $85.00

Sole Proprietor and General Partnership:
- Check your County Recorder and local officials for licenses. You may need to file form TN-1 (trade name) for a cost of $50.00.

Foreign Entities:
- Corporations, limited liability companies, limited partnerships, and other businesses must file forms to transact business in the state. The fees and forms vary. They can be obtained from the Secretary of State's address above.

Tax Registration Requirements

Sales and Withholding Tax:
- No relevant information was supplied by New Hampshire on how to register for either of these taxes. Call the state for information.

In-State Help and Information
- The Business Information Center (BIC) phone number was not listed. Call (202) 205-6665 to see if New Hampshire has set one up yet.
- The SBA Field Office is in Concord, Phone: (603) 225-1400
- Small Business Development Center is at the University of New Hampshire, Durham. Phone; (603) 862-2200.
- Call 1-800-ASK-SBA for SCORE locations.
- Michie's Business Laws Annotated for New Hampshire are $35. To order, call 1-800-562-1197. Web site: *www.michie.com*
- Securities Information: Bureau of Securities Registration, Phone: (603) 271-1463.
- State Web site: *www.state.nh.us*

Notes: Remember that there are several forms and procedures to follow, so consult a lawyer or the state if you do not understand all of them. You can order forms from the State House by calling (603) 271-3244. Cooperatives and professionals have additional requirements.

Source: Secretary of State's Office and Department of Revenue

State Requirements

New Jersey

Secretary of State
Division of Commercial Recording
Trenton, NJ 08625
(609) 530-6400

Division of Taxation
Treasury Dept
PO Box 269
Trenton, NJ 08646-0269
(609) 588-2200

Start-Up Requirements

Business Registration Requirements

Incorporation:
- Reserve a corporate name with the Secretary of State. Cost: $50.00
- File the Original Certificate of Incorporation. File in duplicate or triplicate to be safe. (C-100) Cost: $100.00

Limited Liability Company and Limited Liability Partnership:
- Contact the New Jersey Secretary of State at the address above for information.

Limited Partnership: (1994 Information)
- File a Limited Partnership Certificate, a one-page, two-sided document (LP 100). Cost: $100.00

Sole Proprietor and General Partnership:
- Check with county and local governments.

Foreign Entities:
- Corporations, limited liability companies, limited partnerships, and other businesses must file forms to transact business in the state. The fees and forms vary. They can be obtained from the Secretary of State's address above.

Tax Registration Requirements

Sales and Withholding Tax:
- File Form REG-1, Application for Registration. This will ensure you receive all the forms and information to comply with New Jersey law. Forms will be sent to you to file for sales and withholding after you register with the state. Cost: None

In-State Help and Information
- The Business Information Center (BIC) is in Newark, Phone: (201) 645-6049.
- The SBA Field Office is in Newark, Phone: (201) 645-2434.
- Small Business Development Center is at Rutgers University, Newark. Phone: (201) 648-5950.
- Call 1-800-ASK-SBA for SCORE locations.
- One Stop Capital Shop, Philadelphia, PA. Phone: (215) 790-5005.
- Securities Information: Bureau of Securities, Phone: (201) 504-3620.
- State Web site: *www.state.nj.us*

Notes: Annual reports cost $20.00 for both corporations and limited partnerships. Be sure to check for all other applicable state fees, forms, and requirements for both domestic and foreign entities. New Jersey has an expedited and same-day service for some forms. An additional fee is required for this service.

Source: Secretary of State's Office and Division of Taxation

New Mexico

State Corporation Commission
Corporation Department
PO Drawer 1269
Santa Fe, NM 57504-1269
(505) 827-4511
(505) 827-4504

Taxation and Revenue Dept.
PO Box 25127
Santa, Fe, NM 87504-5127
(505) 827-0700

Start-Up Requirements

Business Registration Requirements

Incorporation: (1994 Information)
- File duplicate originals of the Articles of Incorporation. Cost: $1.00 for each 10,000 shares of stock with a minimum of $50.00.
- File an Affidavit of Acceptance of Appointment by Designated Initial Registered Agent. File duplicate originals. Cost: None listed.

Limited Liability Company and Limited Liability Partnership:
- Contact the New Mexico State Corporation Commission at the address above for information.

Limited Partnership: (1994 Information)
- Reserve a name. Cost: $25.00
- File the certificate of limited partnership with the County Clerk of the county where your principal office is located. Cost: None was listed, write the state.

Sole Proprietor and General Partnership:
- Check your county or city for licensing.

Foreign Entities:
- Corporations, limited liability companies, limited partnerships, and other businesses must file forms to transact business in the state. The fees and forms vary. They can be obtained from the State Corporations Commission's address above.

Tax Registration Requirements

Sales Tax: (1994 Information)
- New Mexico has a Gross Receipts Tax, which is a tax on the privilege of doing business in New Mexico. It is levied on the seller, not the buyer. Write for information on the tax.
- File the Application for Registration to obtain your CRS ID number. Cost: None.

Withholding Tax:
- Contact the New Mexico Taxation and Revenue Department at the address above for information.

In-State Help and Information
- The Business Information Center (BIC) phone number was not listed, call (202) 205-6665 to see if New Mexico has set one up yet.
- SBA Office: Albuquerque, Phone: (505) 766-1870.
- Small Business Development Center, Santa Fe Community College, Santa Fe. Phone: (505) 438-1362.
- Call 1-800-8-ASK-SBA for SCORE locations.
- Securities Information: Securities Division. Phone: (505) 827-7140.

- State Web site: *www.state.nm.us*

Notes: The state was unclear about registering a name beforehand for a corporation, so be sure to check this out. We suggest you pay close attention to your lawyer and the information the state sends you. Limited partnerships should reference Ch 54 NMSA, 1978 compilation regarding their certificates. A copy is available from the Secretary of State for $5.70. The state's revenue department sent a good deal of information, unfortunately, it was disorganized and confusing. We suggest you go to an office to get all of your requirements taken care of.

Source: Secretary of State's Office, State Corporation Commission and Department of Tax. and Revenue

New York

Secretary of State
Dept of State
162 Washington Av
Albany, NY 12231
(518) 473-2492

State Tax Department
WA Harriman Campus
Albany, NY 12227
(518) 474-8275
1-800-225-5829 (Tax Info)
1-800-462-8100 (Forms

Start-Up Requirements

Business Registration Requirements

Incorporation:
- First, send $5.00 and the name you want for your corporation to the Search Unit, Division of Corporations and State Records at the address at above left. Then reserve the name. Cost: $5.00 plus $20.00 for the reservation of the name.
- File a Certificate of Incorporation, which is not available through the state. Go to a legal stationery store or have your lawyer draw up the necessary papers. Cost: $125.00, plus a tax on shares of stock (see NOTES), which is $10.00 minimum. Thus the minimum cost would be $135.00.

Limited Liability Company and Limited Liability Partnership:
- No information sent.

Limited Partnership:
- You may reserve a limited partnership name as above. You must have limited partnership or the abbreviation LP as part of the name. Cost: $20.00 (plus $5.00 for the availability search).
- Execute a partnership agreement and File a Certificate of Limited Partnership with the Secretary of State. Cost: $200.00

Sole Proprietor and General Partnership:
- Nothing needs to be done at the state level; file at the county level.

Foreign Entities:
- Corporations, limited liability companies, limited partnerships, and other businesses must file forms to transact business in the state. The fees and forms vary. They can be obtained from the Secretary of State's address above.

Tax Registration Requirements

Sales Tax:
- File the Application for Registration as a Sales Tax Vendor (DTF-17) and a schedule of Business Locations (DTF-17-ATT). See Publication 750. Cost: None.

Withholding Tax:
- Call the Business Tax Information Center to get a tax profile and preprinted tax forms.

In-State Help and Information
- The Business Information Center (BIC) is in Albany, Phone (518) 446-1118.
- SBA Offices: Buffalo, Phone: (716) 551-4301; Elmira, Phone: (607) 734-8130; Melville, Phone: (516) 454-0750; New York, Phone: (212) 264-1450 and 264-2454; Rochester, Phone: (716) 263-6700; and Syracuse, Phone: (315) 448-0423.
- Small Business Development Center, State University of New York, Albany. Phone: (518) 443-5398.
- Call 1-800-8-ASK-SBA for SCORE locations.
- One Stop Capital Shop, New York. Phone: (212) 866-5640.
- Securities Information: Investors Protection and Securities Bureau. Phone: (212) 416-8209.
- Minority Business Development Agency, New York. Phone: (212) 264-3262.
- State Web site: *www.state.ny.us*

Notes: The tax on corporation's stock is done in the following way. Par value stock is taxed at 1/20 of 1% of total par value. No-par value stock is taxed at 5 cents per share. Remember that the minimum tax, however, is $10.00. Write for tax publications 20 (Tax Guide for New Businesses) and 23 (New Employer Withholding Packet).

Source: Secretary of State's Office and State Tax Department

North Carolina

Secretary of State
300 N Salisbury St
Raleigh, NC 27603
(919) 733-4201

Dept of Revenue
PO Box 25000
Raleigh, NC 27640
(919) 733-3666

Start-Up Requirements

Business Registration Requirements

Incorporation:
- Reserve a corporate name by filing an Application to Reserve a Corporate Name. Cost: $10.00
- File the Articles of Incorporation and one copy with the Secretary of State. Cost: $100.00
- Also, you may need to file an initial franchise tax return with the department of revenue. You may need to file an Application for Privilege License. Call (919) 733-0641 or 1-800-228-8443. Cost: Varies

Limited Liability Company and Limited Liability Partnership:
- No information sent, but there is a Limited Liability Articles of Organization available for download from the Web site.

Limited Partnership: (1994 Information)
- Reserve a name as above to be sure it is not taken. Limited Partnership must be included in the name. Cost: $10.00

- File the Certificate of Domestic Limited Partnership and one copy with the Secretary of State. Cost: $50.00
- You may need to file an Application for Privilege License. Call (919) 733-0641 or 1-800-228-8443. Cost: Varies

Sole Proprietor and General Partnership: (1994 Information)
- Filed at the county level with the Register of Deeds.
- You may need to file an Application for Privilege License. Call (919) 733-0641 or 1-800-228-8443. Cost: Varies

Foreign Entities:
- Corporations, limited liability companies, limited partnerships, and other businesses must file forms to transact business in the state. The fees and forms vary. They can be obtained from the Secretary of State's address above.

Tax Registration Requirements

Sales and Withholding Tax:
- File a Registration Application for Withholding Identification Number, Form AS/RPI. Cost: $15.00 plus $25.00 for an annual wholesale license.

In-State Help and Information
- The Business Information Center (BIC) is in Charlotte, Phone (704) 344-9797.
- SBA Office: Charlotte, Phone: (704) 344-6563.
- Small Business Development Center, University of North Carolina, Raleigh. Phone: (919) 571-4154.
- Call 1-800-8-ASK-SBA for SCORE locations.
- Securities Information: Office of Secretary of State, Securities Division. Phone: (919) 733-3924.
- State Web site:*www.state.nc.us*

Notes: Ask for North Carolina Business Corporation Guidelines. Also, a copy of The Corporation Laws of North Carolina are available from the Michie Company, PO Box 7587, Charlottesville, BA 22906.

Source: Secretary of State's Office and Department of Revenue

North Dakota

Secretary of State
Capitol Building
600 E Boulevard Ave
Bismarck, ND 58505-0599
(701) 328-2900

Tax Commissioner
State Capitol
600 E Boulevard Avenue
Bismarck, ND 58505-0599
(701) 328-2770

Start-Up Requirements

Business Registration Requirements

Incorporation:
- File the Reserve Name Application SFN 13015 (7-93) to reserve your corporate name for one year. Cost: $10.00. You may first call for a search of name record for $5.00.
- File the Articles of Incorporation SFN 16812 (6-89) Cost: $90.00 minimum for the filing, capitalization, and Consent of Registered Agent fees. (See Notes)

- You may also need to file a Trade Name Registration SFN 13401 (10-96) to register your trade name. Cost: $25.00.

Limited Liability Company:
- File the Reserve Name Application SFN 13015 (7-93) to reserve your partnership name for one year. Cost: $10.00. You may first call for a search of name record for $5.00.
- File the Articles of Organization that you write yourself. The state provides you with a guide. Cost: $125.00.
- File the Registered Agent Consent to Serve SFN 7974 (3-95) to register your agent. Cost: $10.00

Limited Partnership:
- File the Filing Certificate. Cost: $100.00 There is no preprinted form.
- File the Reserve Name Application SFN 13015 (7-93) to reserve your partnership name for one year. Cost: $10.00. You may first call for a search of name record for $5.00.
- You may also wish to file a Fictitious Name Certificate. Cost: $25.00.

Sole Proprietor and General Partnership:
- Check the County Recorder. You may wish to file a Trade Name Registration SFN 13401 (10-96) to register your trade name. Cost: $25.00.

Foreign Entities:
- Corporations, limited liability companies, limited partnerships, and limited liability partnerships must file forms to transact business in the state. The fees and forms vary. They can be obtained from the addresses above.

Tax Registration Requirements

Sales Tax:
- File the Application for Sales and Use Tax Permit Form 21869. Cost: None. The sales tax is 2—7% depending on the item sold.

Withholding Tax:
- File the Application to Register for North Dakota Income Tax Withholding Form F-301. Cost: None

In-State Help and Information
- The Business Information Center (BIC) phone number was not listed. Call (202) 205-6665 to see if North Dakota has set one up.
- SBA Office: Fargo, Phone: (701) 239-5131.
- Small Business Development Center, University of North Dakota, Grand Forks. Phone: (701) 777-3700
- Call 1-800-8-ASK-SBA for SCORE locations.
- Department of Economic Development and Finance, Bismarck. Phone: (701) 328-5300.
- One Stop Capital Shop: 1-800-544-4674.
- Securities Information: Securities Commissioner's Office
- State Web site: *www.state.nd.us*

Notes: You will be sent a lot of great forms. Of particular interest is the New Business Registration Forms booklet we received from the tax commissioner. Professional and Cooperative Associations incorporate and form partnerships with different forms, fees, and requirements. The State will send forms and information to you.

Source: Secretary of State's Office and Tax Commissioner

Ohio

Secretary of State
30 E Broad St, 14th Fl
Columbus, OH 43266
(614) 466-3910

Dept of Taxation
PO Box 530
Columbus, OH 43266
(614) 466-4810

Start-Up Requirements

Business Registration Requirements

Incorporation:
- Reserve a corporate name by letter to the Secretary of State. Cost: $5.00
- File Articles of Incorporation, a two page document. In addition, file an Original Appointment of Statutory Agent when you file your Articles. Cost: $85.00 is the minimum fee, based on only 850 shares of stock. The fee goes up for more shares of stock.
- Register shares of stock with the Ohio Department of Commerce, Division of Securities. Cost: $25.00

Limited Liability Company:
- Reserve a name with Secretary of State. Cost: $5.00
- File Articles of Organization with Secretary of State. Cost: $85.00
- File Appointment of Agent for Service of Process. Cost: None

Limited Liability Partnership:
- File registration application with Secretary of State. Cost: $85.00 Annual reports are due in July verifying the information in the registration. Cost: $10.00

Limited Partnership:
- File Certificate of Limited Partnership with Secretary of State. Cost: $85.00

Sole Proprietor and General Partnership:
- Check with the County Recorder. You may need to file a trade name registration or a fictitious name registration.

Foreign Entities:
- Corporations, limited liability companies, limited partnerships, and other businesses must file forms to transact business in the state. The fees and forms vary. They can be obtained from the Secretary of State's address above.

Tax Registration Requirements

Sales Tax:
- File a Regular Vendor's License. Cost: $25.00 plus a $10.00 annual renewal fee. The sales tax is 5% plus up to 3% more for individual counties and transit authorities.

Withholding Tax:
- File Form IT-1 Application for Registration as an Ohio Withholding Agent. Cost: None listed.

In-State Help and Information
- The Business Information Center (BIC) phone number was not listed. Call (202) 205-6665 to see if Ohio has set one up yet.
- SBA Offices: Columbus, Phone: (614) 469-6860; Cincinnati, Phone; (513) 684-2814; Cleveland, Phone: (216) 522-4180.

- Small and Developing Business Division, PO Box 1001, 77 S. High St., Columbus OH 43216. Phone: (614) 466-2711
- Small Business Development Center, Department of Development, Columbus. Phone: (614) 466-2711.
- Call 1-800-8-ASK-SBA for SCORE locations.
- One Stop Business Permit Center for permits. Phone: 1-800-248-4040.
- Securities Information: Division of Securities, Phone: (614) 752-8727.
- State Web site: *www.state.oh.us*

Notes: Write for the Starting Your Business in Ohio booklet, which gives detailed information on starting businesses in Ohio. Booklets to get include Ohio Sales and Use Tax Guide and Ohio's Taxes. An excellent source of start-up kits and permits is the One Stop Business Permit Center. The Small and Developing Business Division has information on business development and minority financing programs.

Source: Secretary of State's Office and Department of Taxation

Oklahoma

Secretary of State
101 State Capitol
Oklahoma City, OK 73105
(405) 521-3911

Tax Commission
2501 N Lincoln Blvd
Oklahoma City, OK 73194
(405) 521-3279

Start-Up Requirements

Business Registration Requirements

Incorporation:
- Reserve a name by filing a name reservation application with the Secretary of State. This holds the name for sixty days.Cost: $10.00
- File the Certificate of Incorporation with the Secretary of State. File in duplicate. Cost: $50.00 minimum. It could be more based on the value of the shares you have. It is $1.00 for each $1000.00 you have of par value stock. No-par value stock is valued at $50.00 per share for determining filing fees only.

Limited Liability Company:
- Reserve a name by filing a name reservation application with the Secretary of State. This holds the name for sixty days.Cost: $10.00
- File the Articles of Organization with the Secretary of State. Cost: $100.00

Limited Partnership:
- Reserve a name by filing a name reservation application with the Secretary of State. This holds the name for sixty days.Cost: $10.00. The name Limited Partnership must appear without abbreviation.
- File the Certificate of Limited Partnership, a one-page, two-sided document. File with the Secretary of State's office in duplicate. Cost: $100.00

Sole Proprietor and General Partnership:
- Check your County Recorder or Clerk and local officials.

Foreign Entities:
- Corporations, limited liability companies, limited partnerships, and other businesses must file forms to transact business in the state. The fees and forms vary. They can be obtained from the Secretary of State's address above.

Tax Registration Requirements

Sales and Withholding Tax:
- To obtain a permit, fill out the Business Registration. Cost: $20.00. Some businesses may have to provide a letter of credit or surety bond. The sales tax in Oklahoma is 4.5%.

In-State Help and Information
- The Business Information Center (BIC) is in Oklahoma City, Phone: (405) 232-1968.
- The SBA Field Office is in Oklahoma City, Phone: (405) 231-5521.
- Small Business Development Center is at Southeast Oklahoma State University, Durant. Phone: (405) 924-0277.
- Call 1-800-ASK-SBA for SCORE locations.
- One Stop Capital Shop, Hugo. Phone (405) 326-6441.
- Securities Information: Department of Securities. Phone: (405) 280-7722.
- State Web site: *www.state.ok.us*

Notes: Oklahoma informed us that engineering, insurance, banking, or farming and ranching must have prior approval from their boards before filing with the Secretary of State. Limited Partnership, without abbreviation, must be in the name of a limited partnership. No information was sent on limited liability partnerships.

Source: Secretary of State's Office and Tax Commission

Oregon

Secretary of State
Corporation Division
255 Capital Street NE
Suite 151
Salem, OR 97310-1327
(503) 986-2222

Dept of Revenue
955 Center St, NE
Salem, OR 97310
(503) 945-8214

Start-Up Requirements

Business Registration Requirements

Incorporation:
- Reserve a name. Cost: $10.00
- File the Articles of Incorporation with the Secretary of State. No minimum capital required. Cost: $50.00, $40.00 for professional corporations.

Limited Liability Company:
- Reserve a name. Cost: $10.00
- File the Articles of Organization. Cost: $40.00

Limited Liability Partnership:
- Reserve a name. Cost: $10.00
- File an Application for Registration. Cost: $40.00

Limited Partnership:
- Reserve a name. Cost: $10.00
- File a Certificate of Limited Partnership with the Secretary of State. Cost: $40.00

General Partnership:
- File an Assumed Business Name Registration. Cost: $10.00 plus $2.00 for each county your business is registered in. Otherwise, check your County Recorder and local government for licenses and registration.

Sole Proprietor:
- File an Assumed Business Name Registration. Cost: $10.00 plus $2.00 for each county your business is registered in. Otherwise, check your County Recorder and local government for licenses and registration.

Foreign Entities:
- Corporations, limited liability companies, limited partnerships, and other businesses must file forms to transact business in the state. The fees and forms vary. They can be obtained from the Secretary of State's address above.

Tax Registration Requirements

Sales Tax:
- Oregon has no sales tax.

Withholding:
- File the Combined Employer's Registration (Form 150-211-055). This will register you for other taxes as well. Cost: None listed. Call the BIC.

In-State Help and Information
- The Business Information Center (BIC) is located in Salem, Phone: (503) 986-2222. Call this office first when you need information.
- The SBA Field Office is in Portland, Phone: (503) 326-2682
- Small Business Development Center is at the Lane Community College, Eugene. Phone: (503) 726-2250.
- Call 1-800-ASK-SBA for SCORE locations.
- Securities Information: Division of Finance and Corporate Securities, Phone: (503) 378-4387.
- State Web site: *www.sos.state.or.us*

Notes: Annual reports are $20.00 for limited partnerships, $30.00 for corporations, and $20.00 for professional corporations. Call the BIC for the excellent Oregon Business Guide. It has all the information you need about business registration. Do not forget local licensing requirements.

Source: Secretary of State's Office and Department of Revenue

Pennsylvania

Sect of the Commonwealth
Department of State
302 N Office Bldg
Harrisburg, PA 17105
(717) 787-7630

Dept of Revenue
Strawberry Sq. 11th Fl
Harrisburg, PA 17101
(717) 787-8201

Start-Up Requirements

Business Registration Requirements

Incorporation:
- Reserve/Register a name. Cost: $52.00
- File the Articles of Incorporation, a one-page, two-sided form with the Department of State, Corporation Bureau. File one original. Cost: $100.00
- In addition, a Docketing Statement in triplicate must accompany the Articles of Incorporation. This registers you with the Departments of State and Revenue. Cost: None

Limited Liability Company and Limited Liability Partnerships:
- Contact the Pennsylvania Secretary of the Commonwealth at the address above for information.

Limited Partnership: (1994 Information)
- File a one-page, two-sided Certificate of Limited Partnership with the Department of State. File one original. Cost: $100.00

Sole Proprietor and General Partnership: (1994 Information)
- No information supplied. Call the Secretary of State or your County Recorder.

Foreign Entities:
- Corporations, limited liability companies, limited partnerships, and other businesses must file forms to transact business in the state. The fees and forms vary. They can be obtained from the Secretary of the Commonwealth's address above.

Tax Registration Requirements

Sales and Withholding Tax:
- File a PA Combined Registration Form PA-100. This registers you for a variety of taxes. Cost: None listed.

In-State Help and Information
- The Business Information Center (BIC) phone number was not listed. Call (202) 205-6665 to see if Pennsylvania has set one up yet.
- The SBA Field Offices are in King of Prussia, Phone: (610) 962-3700; Harrisburg, Phone: (717) 782-3840; Pittsburgh, Phone: (412) 395-6560; and Wilkes-Barre, Phone: (717) 826-6497.
- Small Business Development Center is at the University of Pennsylvania, Philadelphia. Phone: (215) 889-1219.
- Call 1-800-ASK-SBA for SCORE locations.
- One Stop Capital Shop, Philadelphia. Phone (215) 790-5005.
- Securities Information: Securities Commission. Phone: (717) 783-5130.
- Minority Business Development Agency, Philadelphia. Phone: (215) 597-9236.
- State Web site: *www.state.pa.us*

Notes: (1994 Information) Pennsylvania has a fee schedule that may be of interest. In addition, note that you may need to file a form DSCB:17.2, Consent to Appropriation of Name. We were unsure whether this was the same as reserving/registering a name. Check with the Department of State. (Recent Information) Pennsylvania sent us a poor packet of information. All we can tell you is try getting help at an SBA site or through an attorney.

Source: Secretary of the Commonwealth's Office and Department of Revenue

Rhode Island

Secretary of State
270 Westminster Mall
Providence, RI 02903
(401) 277-2357

Division of Taxation
Dept of Administration
One Capitol Hill
Providence, RI 02908-5800
(401) 277-3050

State Requirements

Start-Up Requirements

Business Registration Requirements

Incorporation:
- Call (401) 277-3040 to check on name availability.
- File Application for Reservation of Entity Name, Form 1-9/96. Cost: $50.00
- File Articles of Incorporation, Form No. 11A. Cost: $150.00 for up to $8,000 of stock. It is pro-rated above that.

Limited Liability Company:
- Call (401) 277-3040 to check on name availability.
- File Reservation of Limited Liability Company Name, Form 1/96. Cost: $50.00
- File the Articles of Organization, Forms LLC-1A and LLC-1B (Duplicate Originals). Cost: $150.00.

Limited Liability Partnership:
- Call (401) 277-3040 to check on name availability.
- File the Application for Registered Limited Liability Partnership, Form LLP-1. Cost: $100.00 for each partner, not to exceed $2500.
- Note: This registration must be renewed annually.

Limited Partnership:
- File Application for Reservation of Entity Name, Form 1-9/96. Cost: $50.00
- File Certificate of Limited Partnership, Form LP5A/LP5B. Cost: $100.00.

General Partnership:
- Dealt with at the local city or town level.

Sole Proprietor:
- Register your trade name with your local or town clerk.

Foreign Entities:
- Corporations, limited liability companies, limited partnerships, and other businesses must file forms to transact business in the state. The fees and forms vary. They can be obtained from the Secretary of State's address above.

Tax Registration Requirements

Sales Tax:
- Fill out the Application for Permit to Make Sales at Retail. Cost: $5.00 The sales tax is 7%.

Withholding Tax:
- Call the state. No forms were sent although we do know there is no registration fee.

In-State Help and Information
- The Business Information Center (BIC) is in Providence, Phone: (401) 528-4688.

- The SBA Field Office is in Providence, Phone: (401) 528-4562.
- Small Business Development Center is at Bryant College, Smithfield, Phone: (401) 232-6111.
- Call 1-800-ASK-SBA for SCORE locations.
- First Stop Business Information Center, Phone (401) 277-2185.
- Securities Information: Department of Business Regulations, Securities Division, Phone: (401) 277-3048.
- State Web site: *www.state.ri.us*

Notes: Ask for a copy of the Synopsis of Rhode Island Tax System. Rhode Island's Secretary of State sent an excellent information package, one of the best we received.

Source: Secretary of State's Office and The Division of Taxation

South Carolina

Secretary of State
PO Box 11350
Wade Hampton Bldg
Columbia, SC 29211
(803) 734-2155

SC Tax Commission
301 Gervais St
Columbia, SC 29201
(803) 737-9820

Start-Up Requirements

Business Registration Requirements

Incorporation:
- Reserve a corporate name. Cost: No cost list sent. Write for information.
- File the Articles of Incorporation. Also, file an Initial Annual Report of Corporations. A South Carolina attorney must sign the Articles to certify the corporation was created in accordance to South Carolina code. Cost: $135.00 plus $25.00 for the Initial Annual Report.

Limited Liability Company and Limited Liability Partnership:
- No information sent.

Limited Partnership:
- File the Application for Certificate of Limited Partnership with the Secretary of State. These must be drawn up according to Chapter 25, Title 33, Code of Laws of South Carolina of 1976 and filed in duplicate. Cost: $10.00

Sole Proprietor and General Partnership:
- Check with your county or local city government.

Foreign Entities:
- Corporations, limited liability companies, limited partnerships, and other businesses must file forms to transact business in the state. The fees and forms vary. They can be obtained from the Secretary of State's address above.

Tax Registration Requirements

Sales and Withholding Tax:
- To obtain a retail sales license, fill out form SCTC-111 South Carolina Tax Commission Business Tax Application. This will register you for withholding and other taxes as well. Cost: $50.00.

In-State Help and Information

- The Business Information Center (BIC) is in Charleston, Phone: (803) 853-3900.
- The SBA Field Office is in Columbia, Phone: (803) 765-5377.
- Small Business Development Center is at the University of South Carolina, Columbia, Phone: (803) 777-4907.
- Call 1-800-ASK-SBA for SCORE locations.
- Securities Information: Department of Business Regulations, Securities Division, Phone: (803) 734-1087.
- State Web site: *www.state.sc.us*

Notes: Corporate forms are available at Kitco, Inc. (1-800-351-1244). Not much information was sent to us, so we suggest you write the state for further information and/or publications that may be available.

Source: Secretary of State's Office and SC Tax Commission

South Dakota

Secretary of State
State of South Dakota
500 E Capitol
Pierre, SD 57501-5077
(605) 773-4845

Dept of Revenue
700 Governors Drive
Pierre, SD 57501-2291
(605) 773-5141

Start-Up Requirements

Business Registration Requirements

Incorporation:
- File the Application for Reservation of Name. Cost: $15.00
- File the Articles of Incorporation. Cost: $90.00 minimum for stock of $25,000 or less. It increases thereafter, depending on the value of the stock.

Limited Liability Company:
- File the Application for Reservation of Name. Cost: $15.00
- File the Articles of Organization. Cost: $90.00 minimum, goes up depending on initial capital.

Limited Liability Partnership:
- File the Application for Reservation of Name. Cost: $15.00
- File the Domestic Registration. Cost: $90.00

Limited Partnership:
- File the Application for Reservation of Name. Cost: $15.00
- File a Certificate of Limited Partnership. Cost: $90.00

Sole Proprietor and General Partnership:
- No information sent. Presumably at the county level, though. Call local officials.

Foreign Entities:
- Corporations, limited liability companies, limited partnerships, and other businesses must file forms to transact business in the state. The fees and forms vary. They can be obtained from the Secretary of State's address above.

Tax Registration Requirements

Sales Tax:
- The state recommends visiting one of the field offices for a tax license. Sales tax in South Dakota is 4% plus any applicable city taxes or Indian reservation taxes.

Withholding Tax:
- No information sent. Call the state.

In-State Help and Information
- The Business Information Center (BIC) was not listed, call (202) 205-6665 to see if South Dakota has set one up yet.
- The SBA Field Office is in Sioux Falls, Phone: (605) 330-4231.
- Small Business Development Center is at the University of South Dakota, Vermillion. Phone: (605) 677-5498.
- Call 1-800-ASK-SBA for SCORE locations.
- Securities Information: Department of Commerce and Regulation, Division of Securities, Phone: (605) 773-4823.
- State Web site: *www.state.sd.us*

Notes: Annual reports must be filed by corporations the month the Certificate of Incorporation was issued. The cost is $10.00.

Source: Secretary of State's Office and Department of Revenue

Tennessee

Department of State
Division of Business Services
Suite 1800 James K Polk Bldg.
Nashville, TN 37243-0306
(615) 741-0537

Dept of Revenue
500 Deaderick Street
Andrew Jackson Bldg.
Nashville, TN 37242
(615) 741-2594
1-800-342-1003 (In State)

Start-Up Requirements

Business Registration Requirements

Incorporation:
- File an Application for Reserved Name, form SS-4428. Cost: $20.00 Note, there is also an application for use of indistinguishable name, which you may need to file.
- File a Charter of Incorporation. This is a one page form, number SS-4417. Mail to the Secretary of State. No minimum capital level, although you must list the number of stocks the corporation owns. Cost: $100.00

Limited Liability Company:
- File an Application for Reservation of Name, form SS-4234. Cost: $10.00
- File the Articles of Organization with the Secretary of State. Cost: $50.00 per member at time of filing. However, the minimum fee is $300.00 and the maximum is $3000.00. (Yes, that's right, $3000!)

Limited Liability Partnership:
- File an Application for Reservation of Name, form SS-4487. Cost: $10.00
- File a Certificate of Limited Liability Partnership, form SS-4482. Cost: State did not send it. Call for verification.

Limited Partnership:

- File an application for Reservation of Limited Partnership Name, form SS-4476. Cost: $10.00
- File a Certificate of Limited Partnership with the Secretary of State, form SS-4470. Cost: $50.00

Sole Proprietor and General Partnership:

- Filed at the county and city levels; it costs $20.00 to file new business tax licenses.

Foreign Entities:

- Corporations, limited liability companies, limited partnerships, and other businesses must file forms to transact business in the state. The fees and forms vary. They can be obtained from the Department of State's address above.

Tax Registration Requirements

Sales Tax:

- To obtain a sales tax number, fill out an application for Sales and Use Tax Certificate of Registration. Sales tax rate is 6% with additional local sales taxes. Cost: None

Withholding Tax:

- No information sent.

In-State Help and Information

- The Business Information Center (BIC) is located in Nashville. Phone: (615) 749-4000.
- The SBA Field Office is in Nashville, Phone: (615) 736-5881.
- Small Business Development Center is at the University of Memphis. Phone: (901) 678-2500.
- Call 1-800-ASK-SBA for SCORE locations.
- Securities Information: Securities Division, Department of Commerce and Insurance, Phone: (615) 741-5911.
- State Web site: *www.state.tn.us*

Notes: Write the state for information on foreign businesses, annual reports, and other matters including the filing guides for corporations, limited partnerships, and limited liability companies. The Michie company has a manual on Tennessee business law. Write Michie, PO Box 7587, Charlottesville VA 22906.

Source: Department of States Office and Department of Revenue

Texas

Secretary of State
Corporations Section
PO Box 13697
Austin, TX 78711-3697
(512) 463-5701

Comptroller of Public Accounts
LBJ State Office Bldg
Austin, TX 78774
(512) 463-4000

Start-Up Requirements

Business Registration Requirements

Incorporation:

- Get a preliminary name availability clearance by calling (512) 463-5555. Apply for name reservation. Cost: $40.00
- Create your own Articles of Incorporation, and submit the original and one copy of the Articles of Incorporation to the Secretary of State. The state has a summary listing the minimum requirements for the document. Ask for it. Cost: $300.00
- You must have $1000.00 in issuance of stock as a minimum capital requirement.

Limited Liability Company: (1994 Information)
- File for a limited liability company. Publication Form 205 will be of help with the requirements.

Limited Liability Partnership: (1994 Information)
- File a Registered Limited Liability Partnership. Publication Form 701 will be of help with the requirements.

Limited Partnership: (1994 Information)
- Check on the availability of a name and reserve one. Cost: $75.00
- Certificate of limited partnership as required by the Texas Revised Limited Partnership Act. There are some requirements that the state needs. They will send you a list if you write them. Cost: $750.00

Sole Proprietor and General Partnership: (1994 Information)
- Nothing needs to be filed at the state level, check county and local government.

Foreign Entities:
- Corporations, limited liability companies, limited partnerships, and other businesses must file forms to transact business in the state. The fees and forms vary. They can be obtained from the Secretary of State's address above.

Tax Registration Requirements

Sales Tax:
- To obtain a sales tax permit, fill out the Texas Application, which is for sales tax and use tax. Also, you must post a bond if required (and file an additional form). Cost: None

Withholding Tax:
- Texas has no income tax.

In-State Help and Information
- Business Information Centers (BICs) are in El Paso, Phone: (915) 534-0531; Fort Worth, Phone: (817) 871-6001; and Houston, Phone: (713) 845-2422;
- SBA Offices: Corpus Christi, Phone: (512) 888-3331; Dallas, Phone: (817) 885-6581; El Paso, Phone: (915) 540-5676; Harlingen, Phone: (210) 427-8533; and Houston, Phone: (713) 773-6500.
- Small Business Development Centers: Dallas Community College, Phone: (214) 565-5833; University of Houston, Phone: (713) 752-8444; Texas Tech University, Phone: (806) 745-3973; and University of Texas (San Antonio), Phone: (210) 558-2450.
- Call 1-800-8-ASK-SBA for SCORE locations.
- One Stop Capital Shop, Edinburg. Phone: (210) 316-2610.
- Minority Business Development Agency, Dallas. Phone: (214) 767-8001.
- Securities Information: State Securities Board, Phone: (512) 305-8300.
- Web sites: *www.tax.help@cpa.state.tx.us* and *www.sos.state.tx.us/function/forms*

Notes: You might also have to register your name, which also has a fee. Write the state the find out.

Source: Secretary of State's Office and Comptroller's Office

Utah

Department of Commerce
Division of Corporations
160 East 300 South
Box 146705
Salt Lake City, UT 84114-6705
(801) 530-4849

Tax Commission
210 North 1950 West
Salt Lake City, UT 84134
(801) 297-2200 or
1-800-662-4335

State Requirements

Start-Up Requirements

Business Registration Requirements

Incorporation:
- Submit one original and one copy of the Articles of Incorporation drawn pursuant to state laws and the Department of Commerce Division of Corporations and Commercial Code. Cost: $50.00

Limited Liability Company:
- File the Articles of Organization. Cost: $50.00

Limited Partnership:
- File a Certificate of Limited Partnership. Submit one original and one copy. Cost: $50.00

General Partnership:
- Check for local licenses. Otherwise you may file a DBA (assumed name) for a $20.00 fee for three years.

Sole Proprietor:
- Check for local licenses. Otherwise you may file a DBA (assumed name) for a $20.00 fee for three years.

Foreign Entities:
- Corporations, limited liability companies, limited partnerships, and other businesses must file forms to transact business in the state. The fees and forms vary. They can be obtained from the Department of Commerce's address above.

Tax Registration Requirements

Sales and Withholding Tax:
- File the Utah State Business and Tax Registration form and any other applicable forms. Cost: No Fee

In-State Help and Information
- Business Information Center (BIC) is in Salt Lake City, Phone: (801) 364-1331.
- SBA Office: Salt Lake City, Phone: (801) 524-5800.
- Small Business Development Center: Utah Small Business Development Centers main office, Salt Lake City, Phone: (801) 957-3480. (or *www.slcc.edu/utahsbdc/*)
- Call 1-800-8-ASK-SBA for SCORE locations.
- Securities Information: Department of Commerce, Division of Securities, Phone: (801) 530-6600.

- Division of Business and Economic Development, Salt Lake City. Phone: (801) 538-8889.
- Web site: *www.state.ut.us* and *www.commerce.state.ut.us*

Notes: Ask the Division of Corporations for the excellent guide Doing Business in Utah, a fantastic guide with all the information you will need to start a Utah business. Name searches cost $10.00, and if you need to register your name, it is $20.00. The Tax Commission runs sales and use tax workshops. A form is included in the above listed publication.

Source: Division of Corporations and Commercial Code and Tax Commission

Vermont

Secretary of State
109 State Street
Montpelier, VT 05609-
(802) 828-2386

Department of Taxes
Agency of Administration
1104 109 State Street
Montpelier, VT 05609-1401
(802) 828-2506

Start-Up Requirements

Business Registration Requirements

Incorporation:
- File the Application to Reserve a Name with the Secretary of State. Cost: $20.00
- File the Articles of Incorporation. Cost: $75.00

Limited Liability Company:
- Reserve a name. Cost: $20.00
- File for a Limited Liability Company. Cost: $75.00

Limited Partnership:
- Reserve a name. Cost: $20.00
- File for a Vermont Limited Partnership. Cost: $50.00

Sole Proprietor and General Partnership:
- Nothing at the state level unless you need to register your trade name ($20.00). Check your county or local governments for other requirements.

Foreign Entities:
- Corporations, limited liability companies, limited partnerships, and other businesses must file forms to transact business in the state. The fees and forms vary. They can be obtained from the Secretary of State's address above.

Tax Registration Requirements

Sales and Withholding Tax: (1994 Information)
- File the Registration and Vermont Business Account Number Application, which will register you for several taxes (Form S1). Cost: None

In-State Help and Information
- Business Information Centers (BICs) is in Randolph Center, Phone: (802) 828-4518.
- SBA Office: Montpelier, Phone: (802) 828-4422.
- Small Business Development Center: Vermont Technical College, Randolph Center. Phone: (802) 728-9101.
- Call 1-800-8-ASK-SBA for SCORE locations.

- Securities Information: Securities Division. Phone: (802) 828-3420.
- State Web site: *www.state.vt.us*

Notes: Annual reports are due within two and a half months after the close of the corporate fiscal year (there is no fee now, but legislation is proposed for one). When incorporating, professional corporations also need a certificate from the regulating board of the profession showing that each of the incorporators, directors, and shareholders are licensed to practice in Vermont.

Source: Secretary of State's Office and Department of Taxes

Virginia

Clerks Office
StateCorporation Commission
1300 E. Main Street
Richmond, VA 23219
(804) 371-9733

Dept of Taxation
PO Box 1880
Richmond, VA 23218
(804) 367-8038

Start-Up Requirements

Business Registration Requirements

Incorporation:
- File the Articles of Incorporation (Form SCC 619) with the State Corporation Commission. Cost: Combined Charter Fee and Filing Fee of $75.00 minimum, $2525.00 maximum. See the booklet in Notes for more information.
- Non-stock and professional companies cost the same but use different forms.

Limited Liability Company:
- File the Articles of Organization. Cost: $100.00

Limited Partnership:
- File the Certificate of Limited Partnership (Form LPA-73.11), with the State Corporation Commission. Cost: $100.00

General Partnership:
- Contact the circuit court in the locality wherein business will be conducted.

Sole Proprietor:
- Nothing needs to be done at the state level, check your county authorities.

Foreign Entities:
- Corporations, limited liability companies, limited partnerships, and other businesses must file forms to transact business in the state. The fees and forms vary. They can be obtained from the Clerks Office's address above.

Tax Registration Requirements

Sales and Withholding Tax:
- File form R-1, Combined Registration Application Form for the following taxes: Sales and Use, Employer Withholding, Corporate Income, Litter, Consumer Use, and Tire. The sales tax is 4.5%. Cost: None. You may be liable to file other forms with the Employment Commission as well.

In-State Help and Information

- The Business Information Center (BIC) phone number was not listed. Call (202) 205-6665 to see if Virginia has set one up yet.
- SBA Office: Richmond, Phone: (804) 771-2400.
- Small Business Development Center, Department of Economic Development, Richmond. Phone: (804) 371-8258.
- Securities: Division of Securities and Retail Franchising, Phone: (804) 371-9967
- Call 1-800-8-ASK-SBA for SCORE locations.
- State Web site: *www.state.va.us*

Notes: Write for a copy of the excellent Commonwealth of Virginia Business Registration Guide. It has a wealth of information including flow charts, forms for state and federal requirements, and valuable information. You will also want to contact your local commissioner of revenue or town administrator to determine which local licenses you will need. Another useful publication is the Virginia Corporation Law, available for $20.00 from the Clerk of the State Corporation Commission.

Source: State Corporation Commission and Department of Taxation

Washington

Secretary of State
Corporations Division
2nd Floor, Republic Bldg
505 E Union, PO Box 40234 1-800-647-7706
Olympia, WA 98504-0234
(360) 753-7115

Department of Revenue
PO Box 47450
Olympia, WA 98504

Start-Up Requirements

Business Registration Requirements

Incorporation:
- File a Reservation of Name application. Cost: $30.00
- File the Articles of Incorporation (SSF4) with the Corporations Division of the Secretary of State. Cost: $175.00
- You may be required to file an Annual License Renewal each year for a $59.00 fee.

Limited Liability Company:
- File a Reservation of Name application. Cost: $30.00
- File your original Limited Liability Company filing. Cost: $175.00
- You may be required to file an Initial Annual Report for $10.00

Limited Liability Partnership:
- File a Reservation of Name application. Cost: $30.00
- File an Application for Registration. Cost: $175.00
- You may be required to file an Initial Annual Notice for $50.00. Write for specifics.

General Partnership:
- File a Reservation of Name application. Cost: $30.00
- File an original Limited Partnership filing. Cost: $175.00

Sole Proprietor and General Partnership: (1994 Information)
- File a Master Business Application with the Department of Licensing. Also check your local and county officials for any further licensing.

Foreign Entities:

- Corporations, limited liability companies, limited partnerships, and other businesses must file forms to transact business in the state. The fees and forms vary. They can be obtained from the Secretary of State's address above.

Tax Registration Requirements

Sales Tax:

- Complete and return a Master Business Application for a registration number. Cost: The state did not send information, but we believe it is $15.00. Call the state to find out.

Withholding Tax:

- Washington has no personal income tax.

In-State Help and Information

- The Business Information Centers (BICs) are in Seattle, Phone: (206) 553-7311 and Spokane, Phone: (541) 353-2630.
- SBA Offices: Seattle, Phone: (206) 553-5676; Spokane, Phone: (509) 353-2800.
- Small Business Development Center, Washington State University, Pullman. Phone: (509) 335-1576.
- One Stop Capital Shop, Tacoma. Phone: (206) 274-1288.
- Securities Division, Department of Licensing for stock information, Phone: (360) 902-8760.
- Call 1-800-8-ASK-SBA for SCORE locations.
- State Web site: *www.state.wa.gov*

Notes: Within 120 days of filing Articles of Incorporation, you will need to file an initial annual report. This will be sent to your registered agent. The fee is $10.00. The Revenue Department will send you an excellent New Business Handbook. A special note: businesses must file a business and occupation tax (BandO), which is similar to a "sales" tax. Otherwise there is no corporate taxation.

Source: Secretary of State's Office and Department of Revenue

West Virginia

Secretary of State
State Capitol
Charleston, WV 25305
(304) 558-8000

Dept of Tax and Revenue
Taxpayer's Services Division
PO Box 3784
Charleston, WV 25337-3784
(304) 348-2500

Start-Up Requirements

Business Registration Requirements

Incorporation: (1994 Information)

- First, reserve a corporate name by filing an application. Cost: $15.00 ($30.00 for telephone application)
- File the Articles of Incorporation with the Secretary of State. File duplicate originals. Cost: $90.00 (up to 9,000 shares for minimum fee)

Limited Liability Company and Limited Liability Partnership:

- Contact the West Virginia Secretary of State at the address above for information.

Limited Partnership: (1994 Information)
- File two duplicate originals of the limited partnership agreement. Both must be signed by the general partners. Cost: $10.00 first ten pages, 20 cents each additional page.

Sole Proprietor and General Partnership: (1994 Information)
- Nothing needs to be done at the state level, but you must get a business license. Check your local and county governments.

Foreign Entities:
- Corporations, limited liability companies, limited partnerships, and other businesses must file forms to transact business in the state. The fees and forms vary. They can be obtained from the Secretary of State's address above.

Tax Registration Requirements

Sales Tax: (1994 Information)
- File an Application for Registration Certificate with the Department of Taxation and Revenue. Cost: The form indicated that no remittance was due with the application. However, the completed questionnaire indicated a $15.00 fee. Write for more information.

Withholding Tax:
- No information supplied, but form WV/IT-100.1 is the employer's guide to withholding. Check it out.

In-State Help and Information

- The Business Information Center (BIC) is in Fairmont, Phone: (304) 366-2577.
- SBA Offices: Charleston, Phone: (304) 347-5220; Clarksburg, Phone: (304) 623-5631.
- Small Business Development Center, Governor's Office of Community and Industrial Development, Charleston. Phone: (304) 558-2960.
- Securities Information: Securities Division, Phone: (304) 558-2258.
- Call 1-800-8-ASK-SBA for SCORE locations.
- State Web site: *www.state.wv.gov*

Notes: There is also a Corporate License Tax for corporations: minimum fee of $20.00.

Source: Secretary of State's Office and Department of Taxation and Revenue

Wisconsin

Department of Financial Institutions
Division of Corporate and
Consumer Services
PO BOX 7846
Madison, WI 53707-7846
(608) 261-9555 or
(608) 266-3590

Department of Revenue
PO Box 8933
Madison, WI 53708-8933
(608) 266-1911

Start-Up Requirements

Business Registration Requirements

Incorporation:

- File the Name Reservation Application DFI/CCS/Corp Form 1 to reserve your corporate name. Cost: $15.00.
- File the Articles of Incorporation DFI/CCS/Corp Form 2 with the Secretary of State. Cost: $90.00. This is for up to 9,000 shares. Add 1 cent for each authorized share in excess of that.
- File the Statement of Newly Elected Officers and Directors DFI/CCS/Corp Form 20 if you change any of the principal officers. Cost: $3.00. Not all corporations need to file this, so check with the State.
- An annual report is due and costs $25.00 to file.

Limited Liability Company:

- File the Name Reservation Application DFI/CCS/Corp Form 1 to reserve your corporate name. This lasts 120 days and can be renewed with another form. Cost: $15.00.
- File the Articles of Organization (Limited Liability Company) DFI/CCS/Corp Form 502. Cost: $130.00.

Limited Partnership:

- File the Name Reservation Application DFI/CCS/Corp Form 1 to reserve your corporate name. This lasts sixty days and can be renewed with another form. Cost: $10.00.
- File the Certificate of Limited Partnership DFI/CCS/Corp Form 302. Cost: $70.00

Limited Liability Partnership:

- File the Registration Statement for Limited Liability Partnerships DFI/CCS/Corp Form 602. Cost: $100.00.
- You may have other forms to file. The State information was sketchy on this, so call or write for more information.

Sole Proprietor and General Partnership:

- No information sent. Check with the County Recorder or clerk. You may need to register your company and/or obtain a business license.

Foreign Entities:

- Corporations, limited liability companies, limited partnerships, and limited liability partnerships must file forms to transact business in the state. The fees and forms vary. They can be obtained from the Department of Financial Institutions' address above.

Tax Registration Requirements

Sales Tax:

- File an Application for Permit (Form A-101). Cost: $5.00 per location. Form S-207 is the Certificate of Exemption. Write the state for information.

Withholding:

- File the form in W-166 Wisconsin Employer's Withholding Tax Guide. You will receive a withholding registration certificate. Cost: None listed.

In-State Help and Information

- The Business Information Center (BIC) phone number was not listed. Call (202) 205-6665 to see if Wisconsin has set one up.
- SBA Field Offices are in Madison, Phone: (608) 264-5261 and Milwaukee, Phone: (414) 297-3941.

- Small Business Development Center, University of Wisconsin, Madison. Phone: (608) 263-7794
- Call 1-800-8-ASK-SBA for SCORE locations.
- Securities Information: Securities/Franchise Investment, Registration Division, Phone: (608) 266-3431.
- State Web site: *www.dor.state.wi.us*

Notes: You may expedite many of these procedures by using the phone or paying expedition fees. Check with the State. The corporation commences at the time and date received by the state. You may be required to post a security deposit before your seller's permit is issued. You may also need to file a Certificate or Statement of Status, but you can request that information from the State.

Sources: DFI Division of Corporate and Consumer Services and Department of Revenue

Wyoming

Secretary of State
State Capitol Building
Cheyenne, WY 82002
(307) 777-7311
(307) 777-7312

Dept of Revenue
122 W. 25th St
Cheyenne, WY 82002-0110
(307) 777-7961

Start-Up Requirements

Business Registration Requirements

Incorporation: (1994 Information)
- Reserve a trade name for 120 days. Cost: $30.00
- File the Articles of Incorporation, a one-page, two-sided document. Cost: $100.00
- A written consent to appointment by the registered agent must accompany the Articles.

Limited Liability Company and Limited Liability Partnership:
- Contact the Wyoming Secretary of State at the address above for information.

Limited Partnership: (1994 Information)
- Reserve a trade name as above. Cost: $5.00 plus $10.00 to file.
- In addition to, or instead of (the information was unclear), Reserve a Limited Partnership name for $3.00.
- Execute a certificate of limited partnership in accordance with Wyoming requirements. Submit in duplicate originals. Cost: $50.00 minimum fee, $2,500.00 maximum fee. This changed in 1993, however. Check the state for appropriate new fees.

Sole Proprietor and General Partnership:
- Contact the Wyoming Secretary of State at the address above for information.

Foreign Entities:
- Corporations, limited liability companies, limited partnerships, and other businesses must file forms to transact business in the state. The fees and forms vary. They can be obtained from the Secretary of State's address above.

Tax Registration Requirements

Sales Tax: (1994 Information)

- File an application for Sales and Use Tax License. Cost: $150.00 must be deposited as a condition of licensing. Tax is credited against future collections.
- The state has no income tax and therefore no withholding.

In-State Help and Information

- The Business Information Center (BIC) phone number was not listed. Call (202) 205-6665 to see if Wyoming has set one up.
- SBA Field Office is in Casper, Phone: (307) 261-5761.
- Small Business Development Center, University of Wyoming, Laramie. Phone: (307) 766-3505.
- Securities Information: Secretary of State's Office, Phone: (307) 777-5347.
- Call 1-800-8-ASK-SBA for SCORE locations.
- State Web site: *www.state.wy.us*

Notes: Wyoming has no personal income tax and no corporate income tax, just a report license tax, which is pleasantly low. The state portrays itself as "pro-business", and the information we received seemed to definitely confirm this. Write the state for their excellent business entity package, which consisted of several useful publications.

Source: Secretary of State's Office and Department of Revenue and Taxation

As a final reminder, remember that there may be other requirements you need to look into, or that some requirements may change as states enact new laws or overhaul old bureaucratic systems. Be sure, therefore, to write your state *first* and get all the facts. This way, you can be sure. Also, do not forget local regulations. Your lawyer can tell you about them, as can your County Recorder, City Clerk or County Clerk, local incubator, city government, or Chamber of Commerce.

Conclusion

By this time, you have learned three practical things. One, just what type of legal entity you should become; two, how to go about be coming it; and three, how to support your new business with financial aid and technical expertise. You also know that the most important thing you can have—initially—is motivation. Further, you know that research, a good business plan, and the proper organization type are crucial for your success.

How well you utilize the information in this book is up to you. But consider this. You want to start a business, you want to be your own boss, chart your own destiny. Remember earlier we said that in the United States, nearly a million new businesses are started each year. Well, many fail for a variety of reasons. But many succeed. Why? Because they are the ones who research, plan, and set reasonable business and personal goals. They are the ones who keep good records, maintain positive cash flows, and work hard. The others are so busy trying to run that they never learn to walk.

So by reading this guide, you should be ready to get off to a good start, and on the right foot, too. That is one of the most important things we can tell you. But do not forget, that once off the ground, you must run the business. That is when it is time for other books on how to run a business. We hope that this book is helpful in starting your business, and that others will be helpful in running your business.

The following appendixes contain a list of SBA publications, state tax rates, and a comprehensive worksheet. All of these should be of assistance to you, especially during your research phase.

Remember, the only way you can be your own boss is by going for it: by starting your business. That, after all, is the first step toward your dream. Good Luck!

Small Business Administration Publications

These are available from the SBA and cost $2-$3 for publications and up to $39 for videos. Write the SBA for more information and publication descriptions.

Emerging Business Series
  Transferring Management/Family Business
  Marketing Strategies for Growing Businesses
  Management Issues for Growing Businesses
  Human Resource Management for Growing Businesses
  Audit Checklist for Growing Businesses
  Strategic Planning for Growing Businesses

Financial Management for Growing BusinessesFinancial Management
  ABCs of Borrowing
  Understanding Cash Flow
  A Venture Capital Primer for Small Business
  Budgeting in a Small Service Firm
  Record Keeping in a Small Business
  Pricing Your Products and Services Profitably
  Financing for Small Business

Management and Planning
  Problems in Managing a Family-Owned Business
  Business Plan for Small Manufacturers
  Business Plan for Small Construction Firms
  Planning and Goal Setting for Small Business
  Business Plan for Retailers
  Business Plan for Small Service Firms
  Checklist for Going into Business
  How to Get Started with a Small Business Computer
  Business Plan for Home-Based Business
  How to Buy or Sell a Business
  Developing a Strategic Business Plan
  Inventory Management
  Selecting the Legal Structure for Your Business
  Evaluating Franchise Opportunities
  Small Business Risk Management Guide
  Child Day-Care Services
  Handbook for Small Business
  How to Write a Business Plan

Marketing

Creative Selling: The Competitive Edge
Marketing for Small Business: An Overview
Researching Your Market
Selling by Mail Order
Advertising

Products/Ideas/Inventions

Ideas into Dollars
Avoiding Patent, Trademark, and Copyright Problems

Personnel Management

Employees: How to Find and Pay Them

Videotapes

Marketing: Winning Customers with a Workable Plan
The Business Plan: Your Road Map to Success
Promotion: Solving the Puzzle
Home-Based Business: A Winning Blueprint
Basics of Exporting

Miscellaneous

U.S. Government Purchasing and Sales Directory

Appendix B

State Tax Rates

State	Sales Tax	Corporate Tax Rates
Alabama	4.00%	5.00%
Alaska	None	1.00%–9.40%
Arizona	5.00%	9.00%
Arkansas	4.50%	1.00%–6.50%
California	6.00%	9.30%
Colorado	3.00%	5.00%
Connecticut	6.00%	10.75%
District of Columbia	5.75%	9.975%
Delaware	None	8.70%
Florida	6.00%	5.50%
Georgia	4.00%	6.00%
Hawaii	4.00%	4.40%–6.40%
Idaho	5.00%	8.00%
Illinois	6.25%	4.80%
Indiana	5.00%	7.90%
Iowa	5.00%	6.00%–12.00%
Kansas	4.90%	4.00%
Kentucky	6.00%	4.00%–8.25%
Louisiana	4.00%	4.00%–8.00%
Maine	6.00%	3.50%–8.93%
Maryland	5.00%	7.00%
Massachusetts	5.00%	9.50%
Michigan	6.00%	2.30%
Minnesota	6.50%	9.80%
Mississippi	7.00%	3.00%–5.00%
Missouri	4.225%	6.25%
Montana	None	6.75%
Nebraska	5.00%	5.58%–7.81%
Nevada	6.50%	None
New Hampshire	None	7.00%
New Jersey	6.00%	9.00%
New Mexico	5.00%*	4.80%–7.60%
New York	4.00%	9.00%
North Carolina	4.00%	7.75%
North Dakota	5.00%	3.00%–10.50%
Ohio	5.00%	5.28%–8.90%
Oklahoma	4.50%	6.00%
Oregon	None	6.60%
Pennsylvania	6.00%	9.99%
Rhode Island	7.00%	9.00%
South Carolina	5.00%	5.00%
South Dakota	4.00%	None
Tennessee	6.00%	6.00%
Texas	6.25%	4.50%
Utah	5.00%	5.00%
Vermont	5.00%	5.50%–8.25%
Virginia	4.50%	6.00%
Washington	6.50%	None
West Virginia	6.00%	9.00%
Wisconsin	5.00%	7.90%
Wyoming	4.00%	None

* Gross Receipts Tax Rate   All Numbers for 1996

Worksheet: Vital Start-Up Information

Complete this worksheet as you attain this information. Some of it you can fill in before you start your business, such as names and addresses. Other information will become available as you file forms and go through the bureaucracy.

Company Name: _____

    Address: _____

    City/State/Zip: _____

    Phone: _____

Check the box that applies to your business and fill in the information.

☐ Corporation   State of Incorporation:_____

Registered Agent:_____Phone:_____

    Address: _____

    City/State/Zip: _____

President:_____Phone:_____

    Address: _____

    City/State/Zip: _____

Vice-
President:_____Phone:_____

    Address: _____

    City/State/Zip: _____

Secretary:_____Phone:_____

    Address: _____

    City/State/Zip: _____

Treasurer:_____Phone:_____

    Address: _____

    City/State/Zip: _____

    Assumed/Trade/DBA Name:_____

Shares of stock:_____ Number of Stockholders:_____

Type of stock:_____ Value of stock:_____

Type of corporation: ☐ Corporation   ☐ S-Corporation

☐ Limited Liability Company

Registered
Agent:_____Phone:_____

    Address: _____

    City/State/Zip: _____

Officer:_____Phone:_____

    Address: _____

    City/State/Zip: _____

Officer:_____Phone:_____

    Address: _____

    City/State/Zip: _____

Officer:_____Phone:_____

    Address: _____

    City/State/Zip: _____

Officer:_____Phone:_____

    Address: _____

    City/State/Zip: _____

    Assumed/Trade/DBA Name:_____

☐ General Partnership

☐ Written Partnership Agreement Attached

General Partner:_____Phone:_____

    Address: _____

    City/State/Zip: _____

General Partner:_____Phone:_____

    Address: _____

    City/State/Zip: _____

    Assumed/Trade/DBA Name:_____

☐ Limited Partnership

☐ Written Partnership Agreement Attached

General Partner:_____Phone:_____

    Address: _____

    City/State/Zip: _____

General Partner:_____Phone:_____

    Address: _____

    City/State/Zip: _____

Limited Partner:_____Phone:_____

    Address: _____

    City/State/Zip: _____

☐ Sole Proprietor

Sole Proprietor: _____

☐ Tax Information

    Federal ID number:_____ (FEIN or FIN)

    State sales tax exemption number:_____

    Tax accounting period (month, year):_____

    Accounting Procedure: ☐ Single Entry ☐ Double Entry

    Number of Employees:_____

        Tax Forms Needed

        W-2 Forms: _____

        W-4 Forms: _____

        1099 forms: _____

        Sales Tax: _____ (Remittance Forms)

        Coupon Bks: _____(Federal Tax Coupon
        Remittance Book 8109)

    Others:_____

    _____

    _____

☐ Licenses

License:_____

License:_____

License:_____

License:_____

☐ Local Permits

Permits:_____

Permits:_____

Permits:_____

Permits:_____

☐ Insurance Needs

    Liability

    Worker's Compensation

    Health Care

Business Continuation
Property/Casualty
Life (Yourself and employees)
Automobile
Crime Insurance
Bonding (If needed. You may also list it under Licenses)

Agents:_____

Agents:_____

    Address: _____

    City/State/Zip: _____

    Phone: _____

☐ Banking Information

Needs:

      ☐ Checking Account Number:_____

      ☐ Savings Account Number:_____

      ☐ Payroll Services:_____

      ☐ Billing Services:_____

      ☐ Loans—Outstanding Loans:_____

Banker: _____

Bank: _____

Address: _____

City/State/Zip: _____

Phone: _____

☐ Software and Hardware

    Word processing software:

      ☐ Word   ☐ WordPerfect Other:_____

    Spreadsheets and Accounting:

      ☐ Excel   ☐ Lotus ☐ Peachtree Other:_____

Databases:

☐ FoxPro ☐ Access DbaseIII   Other:_____

Misc: (Such as billing, form creation and industry specific software)

Other:_____Other:_____

Other:_____Other:_____

Hardware:

☐ Computer Make:_____

☐ Printer Make:_____

☐ Fax/Modem:
Internal or Enternal Make:_____

Internet:

☐ Internet Site:_____

☐ E-Mail address:_____

Index